A Pilgrimage to the Land of the Saints

a self-guided retreat
following the journey of Saint Brendan the Navigator

by
Timothy J. Ray

For as the rain and the snow come down from heaven,
and do not return there until they have watered the earth,
        making it bring forth and sprout,
giving seed to the sower and bread to the eater,
so shall my word be that goes out from my mouth;
        it shall not return to me empty,
but it shall accomplish that which I purpose,
and succeed in the thing for which I sent it.

Isaiah 55: 10-11

Table of Contents

A Pilgrimage to the Land of the Saints:
A self-guided retreat

Returning Home

Resources for Private Prayer

Preface

an Ignatian journey with a Celtic pilgrim

Guided by the readings and prayer services of *A Voyage to the Land of the Saints*, the retreat presented in this book invites you to observe or participate in the events of Brendan's pilgrimage — as well as related episodes from the Scriptures — through the use of centuries-old techniques of imaginative prayer. Developed by Ignatius of Loyola in the 16th century, the methods of prayer used in this book will allow you to join Brendan and his companions on their adventures while considering how aspects of their travels mirror your own spiritual life. This imaginary journey of prayerful exploration will reveal God's pervasive presence in you and in the world around you as well as your responses to it.

It might be tempting to dismiss the imagination as whimsy, but I have learned — in situations ranging from personal prayer to community-wide conversations — that imaginative exercises liberate us to consider the possibilities lying dormant in our lives. Precisely because it is not real, the playfulness of the imagination allows us to express our deepest desires and to experiment with potential realities without risking deleterious consequences. But imaginary worlds can become seductive and isolate us from reality, so it remains important that we consider the ways that the fruits of our imagination enhance our day-to-day lives rather than remove us from them.

With these concerns in mind, the retreat presented in this book extends and deepens (through the active — but careful — use of your imagination) what I described in the preface to *A Voyage to the Land of the Saints* as "a personal encounter with the unique form of spiritual testimony exemplified in the legend of Brendan's pilgrimage." The techniques of imaginative contemplation developed by Ignatius of Loyola will help you foster an intimate conversation with God while entering the events of Brendan's pilgrimage and episodes from the Gospel of St. John as well as playfully engaging your five senses to heighten your sensitivity to the nuances of these experiences. But, at every stage in your journey, you will be asked to review your prayers (and the events surrounding them) in order to help you understand the spiritual desires and temptations being evoked in you as well as the practical choices being offered to you.

Through your journey with Brendan during your retreat, it is my hope that (as I explained in the preface to this book's companion volume) "you will experience the presence of God in your own life and the invitation to seek out your own particular place of resurrection." In whatever form it takes — physical, metaphorical or spiritual — pilgrimage involves an active and highly personal choice to travel toward the sacred in our own lives and in the world around us. It requires that we reconcile the interior silence of contemplative prayer (needed to discern God's presence in our lives) with the practical day-to-day demands of engaging the people or causes that God invites us to serve. Each of us must resolve this tension in our own distinctive way, shaping a unique identity that balances contemplation with action as well as individuality with community. So, you should recognize that this retreat serves as the beginning of a larger spiritual journey.

In following Brendan to his place of resurrection, and then striving to discern your own, you are opening yourself to a life-long journey. As Ignatius of Loyola asserts in a one of his letters, "We must always remind ourselves that we are pilgrims until we arrive at our heavenly homeland, and we must not let our affections delay us in the roadside inns and lands through which we pass, otherwise we will forget our destination and lose interest in our final goal." This is a journey that requires the same trust in God's guidance and protection that Brendan and his companions demonstrated when they set out on their own pilgrimage to the Land of the Saints.

Still, at each step along the way of your coming journey, you should remember that you are in the care of a loving God who sends his Spirit to guide you and his Son to companion you. During your retreat, God will provide the spiritual gifts you need to understand your role in his plan of redemption. After the retreat, he will nourish these gifts as they take root in you. So, in this knowledge of God's providence, you should approach the retreat with a playful passivity that relies on your imagination to listen to what God has to say to you before embarking on a more active process of discernment after the retreat using the resources in this book designed to help you when you return home.

So, as you prepare to set out with Brendan and his companions on their pilgrimage to the Land of the Saints, may the following words from The Wisdom of Solomon sustain your confidence in the love and care God constantly bestows upon you:

"It is your providence, O Father, that steers

[a craft on] its course,
because you have given it a path in the sea,
and a safe way through the waves,
showing that you can save from every danger,
so that even a person who lacks skill may put to sea."
Chapter 14: 3-4

Thanks and Acknowledgements

This book represents a personal journey that would not have been possible without the companionship of J. L. Chapman, Bernard Colonna, John Dale, Kathleen Deignan, Edward Egros, Rosalyn Knowles Ferrell, Ruben Habito, Patrick Henry, Per Mollerup, Susan Rakoczy, Brian Ramsay and David Teschner. To varying degrees, and for different lengths of time, the support and encouragement of these friends helped me persevere in this pilgrimage.

Also, in a very special way, I would like to thank James Swonger for his generous assistance in designing and creating the digital audio components of this project as well as for a friendship that began long before this journey with Brendan and his companions.

In addition, I am grateful for:
• the permission of Padraic Colum's estate to excerpt his "The Burial of Saint Brendan" from *The Poet's Circuits: collected poems of Ireland* (Dublin: Dolmen Press, 1981).
• the permission of *The Capuchin Annual* and the King estate to reproduce Richard King's image of Saint Brendan on the cover of this book.

Finally, I would like to acknowledge the invaluable contributions to this book of Alexander Carmichael's compilation of Gaelic prayers in *Carmina Gadelica: Hymns and Incantations* (Edinburgh: Floris Books, 1992). The prayers in this public domain collection offer intimate expressions of personal faith but the language of these translations may occasionally distract modern readers from this fact. So, while preserving the poetic nature of these prayers, some of their language has been revised in this book to reflect contemporary English usage.

Building a Vessel for your Pilgrimage

Before beginning this journey with Brendan and his companions, you should consider the resources gathered in this book and how they might best be used to help you in your spiritual travels.

Building a Vessel for Your Pilgrimage

considerations on using the materials in this book

For Brendan and his companions, a pilgrimage was an open-ended voyage. They did not know how long their journey would be, only that God would guide them. This profound confidence in God — and openness to God's desires — also should mark your approach to this book, which offers the resources for a personal pilgrimage of the imagination that follows the voyage of Brendan and his companions. You need to trust that God will help you decide whether to use these materials to make a retreat in the midst of your daily activities or by going into seclusion for a time as well as whether you want to pray alone or with others. You also need to recognize and trust that God will help sustain your efforts once these decisions are made. Remember that pilgrimage is an act of faith in which you place every aspect of your life in God's care.

Yet, this trust in God's support and guidance does not annul your responsibility to prepare for your pilgrimage. Brendan and his companions needed to build and stock a vessel for their journey to the Land of the Saints, a sailing boat made of wood and animal hides well-suited to their long ocean voyage. So, your preparation should be no less rigorous as you assemble the resources necessary to protect and sustain your own spiritual odyssey. This means deciding the type of spiritual journey you wish to make before crafting your own prayerful vessel from the time, places and conversations you are willing to commit to your pilgrimage. It also requires that you give careful thought to the length of your voyage and the risks you are willing to take on it. Finally, consider whether you wish to make this pilgrimage alone or whether you want to invite companions to join you during your travels.

A Pilgrimage to the Land of the Saints
a self-guided retreat, in daily life or in seclusion

This self-guided retreat creates an intensely intimate spiritual journey with Brendan and his companions. The readings from *The Voyage of Saint Brendan*, their companion meditations and related scriptural passages — presented through the prayer services in *A Journey to the Land of the Saints* — introduce the retreat's themes but

Ignatian spiritual practices shape the methods of prayer used during the retreat. Like the Celtic tradition of Saint Brendan, Ignatian spirituality asserts that God is present in all of his creation and wants to communicate with us so we may shape our lives in harmony with his desires. To help men and women hear the voice of God more clearly, Ignatian prayer engages the imagination to place individuals in the events at the center of their prayer and encourages them to review God's activity in their lives through a short daily prayer called the examen. These simple methods of prayer come easily to most people, providing a profound awareness of God's presence in us and in the world around us once they have been mastered.

As you prepare for your retreat, it is important for you to consider the desires you bring to your spiritual journey. You will be able to complete this retreat either through nine days of secluded prayer or over nine weeks in daily life. When praying in seclusion, there is relatively little time between formal prayers and the presence of God permeates your consciousness — making every moment an encounter with the sacred. On the other hand, when praying in daily life, your formal prayer becomes the focal point of your day as it draws your mundane activities into a sacred space within your consciousness. Whether in seclusion or in daily life, you also may choose to make your retreat alone or in the company of others. So, you should take some time to consider the possibilities and requirements of each of these choices.

If you decide to make the retreat in daily life, you will need to do everything possible to separate your prayers from your daily routine. It will be very important for you to be able to release yourself from your day-to-day concerns and problems — and to make certain that none of your daily activities tire or overstimulate you — before entering prayer. You should separate your place and time of prayer from any distractions, creating a special place where you will pray and developing personal practices that mark the transition from daily life into your special time of prayer — perhaps using one of the rituals described in "On Holy Ground" in the resources section at the end of this book. Once you have made these choices, you will need to pay very careful attention to being consistent in your prayer.

During the retreat in daily life, you should dedicate approximately one-and-a-half hours of each day to prayer. You should devote 45 to 50 minutes every day to either the preparation exercises, the formal contemplations, or the review of the week's prayer (following the weekly order described in the introduction to the retreat). Also, you should spend an additional 10 minutes reviewing those periods involving imaginative prayer as soon afterward as possible (even if you prepare only brief notes) so your later reflections remain fresh and clear. Finally, at the beginning and end of your day, you should set aside 15 minutes for each of the examens. For the sake of consistency, and to foster an awareness that all of these activities are special moments with God, you should commit the same times each day to your different prayers — selecting them carefully so you are able to relax and put aside your other concerns in a regular daily rhythm.

Note: _Like Brendan and his companions, you should travel as lightly as possible during your spiritual pilgrimage and trust that God will guide you to the place he has prepared for you. Do not allow your prayers or reflections to become burdensome — or exhausting — by adding more time to your prayers (even when it feels pleasant) or spending too much time on your reflections (since it may take you "into your head")._

The place you pray during the daily life retreat may be more flexible than the time, but it remains important that you consecrate a special space for prayer and preserve its distinctive character. You may create a comfortable and contemplative atmosphere in your home by dedicating a specific area — either a room or a portion of a room — as a prayer space, providing a focal point in this place (e.g., a statue, icon or cross with a few candles) and muted lighting that helps quiet both you and it. Or you may decide to pray in an existing prayer room or chapel at a nearby church. You also may choose to alternate between prayer spaces that are inside or outside your home, as long a you remain consistent in using a particular place on a specific day to preserve the rhythm of your prayer.

However, if you choose to make this retreat in seclusion, this spiritual rhythm will be sustained by the consistency of your prayer. Your four or five daily conversations with God will dominate your retreat, with each period devoting 45 to 50 minutes to imaginative contemplation and 10 minutes to the preliminary review of your prayer. So, you will need to remove any impediments to these times of prayer so they become consistent events in your day. To heighten your sensitivity to the emotional and spiritual undercurrents of these special moments, you may find it useful to integrate the examens into your preparation for prayer in the morning or the review of your prayer at the end the day — focusing your attention on the desires you bring to your prayer and God's response to them.

Just as you must prepare a time of stillness for your prayer, it also will be important for you to create a calm environment for your time in seclusion. Depending on whether you decide to make your retreat at home or somewhere else, you will face different types of obstacles. At home, you will need to create a silent space for your prayer by selecting places to pray as well as making friends and neighbors aware of your need for privacy as you take some time to be alone. Away from home, you will need to make arrangements to create the stillness you will need during your retreat. In either case, it would be good to have access to quiet and beautiful places during your retreat (e.g., parks, beaches, woodlands, etc.) where you might choose to pray or simply spend quiet time between prayer periods.

If you decide to make a secluded retreat at home, you also will need to curtail your normal daily activities and limit your contact with other people. You should preserve activities that you find restful or reflective while putting aside any pursuits that distract or tire you. If you do not like cooking, for example, you should arrange for your main meal to be delivered to you or plan simple meals that require little preparation. Activities you enjoy but which might tire you (e.g., exercise, physical labor, etc.) will need to be moderated and any daily habits which provoke their own emotions, thoughts and reflections (e.g., reading, listening to the radio, watching television, etc.) will need to be suspended. Also, inform anyone who might contact you that you will be unavailable and leave a message to this effect on all your devices. Finally, you should arrange for someone to receive emergency messages for you during the retreat.

But, if you do not feel comfortable praying so intensely at home, you may decide to make the retreat while camping (if this is restful for you) or by checking into an inn or bed-and-breakfast during the retreat. While camping provides its own isolation and silence, you will need to tell the management of an inn about your plan and ask to be given a certain amount of privacy. If it offers meals, for example, ask that a small table be set aside for you or that your meals be brought to your room. You also will need to tell housekeeping not to disturb you during your stay, arranging to change linens at times that are least disruptive to your retreat. Finally, since you are in an unfamiliar place, you should bring some small prayer objects to use as focal points during your retreat.

Note: The introduction to the retreat contains suggested
schedules for making the retreat in daily life or in seclusion as well as
considerations of other concerns you need to address before beginning
your retreat — choosing a Bible translation, pacing your prayer, and
suggestions on various aspects of prayer during the retreat.

After deciding how you want to approach the retreat, whether in
daily life or in seclusion, you should consider whether the
companionship of others would enrich your prayer or detract from it. If
you make this retreat in solitude, your retreat experience will be
completely self-determined and private since you will decide when and
where you wish to pray. With others, you will have the prayerful
support of your companions but you will need to be flexible in allowing
them to have their own spiritual experience. In either case, the retreat
will be an intense and personal encounter with God. So, after making
an honest appraisal of your desires, and after separating these desires
from any outside influences (including your friendship with potential
companions), you should decide whether God is asking you to pray in
solitude or in the company of friends.

If you choose to make your spiritual pilgrimage with others, you
will need to be certain that each individual's needs for the retreat —
both spiritual and material — are fulfilled. You should gather your
companions to discuss your various hopes and desires for the retreat,
paying careful attention to the amount of time that each of you wants
to spend in prayer and the places where each of you prefers to pray. In
your discussions, you should push your collective spiritual experience
to the limit of its potential while still protecting each member of your
group from feeling pressured beyond their capabilities.

Including spiritual companions on your retreat may be simpler
when you are making the retreat in daily life. If a local church or prayer
group is offering the sequence of prayer services from *A Journey to the
Land of the Saints*, you and your companions could attend that service
together at the beginning of each "week" of the retreat and pray
separately until the next prayer service. If not, you will need to find (or
create) a location where you and your companions may conduct your
own services — a chapel or prayer room at a local church or a
temporary space in the home of one of your companions. This place
should be large enough for all of you to gather comfortably for the

services but also intimate enough for private prayer in case any members of your group wish to use it during the retreat.

However, if your group decides to make a secluded retreat away from home, you should select a quiet place that allows each of you to focus on your individual prayer. This might be a place that cares for your material needs — such as a retreat house, a conference center, or a small inn — or it might be a cabin or vacation home where you provide for your own needs. As you select this place, be certain that it addresses the concerns discussed earlier in creating a contemplative environment for private prayer as well as offers ample space for your shared prayer during the retreat. Also, remember that you and your companions will need the space and freedom to find God in your own individual rhythms, both in formal periods of prayer and in the quiet time in between, so carefully select a place that sustains each of you on your shared voyage with Brendan and his companions.

You also need to discuss the practical concerns of being together in this new environment. To avoid intruding on each other's prayer, you should maintain silence for as much of the retreat as possible. So, you should decide ahead of time how much of your time together will be silent. You also need to discuss how your group will handle living accommodations, personal daily routines and any chores that might arise (e.g., preparing or setting out meals). In addition to these concerns, you should discuss ways to resolve any conflicts that might arise when members of your group find themselves attracted to the same prayer spaces at the same time during the retreat. In all these matters, be generous with each other and your respective needs as friends on a shared journey.

Note: Before making your decisions about making the retreat with companions, be certain to include the considerations from the introduction to the retreat in your preparatory conversations. Also, if you are planning on using the prayer services during your prayer together, take time to review the issues discussed in the introduction to the prayer services in A Journey to the Land of the Saints.

Whether you make the retreat in daily life or seclusion — alone or with companions — you should keep a journal of your experiences since this retreat represents an extended voyage with Christ. Many of the benefits of the retreat will become evident in the months after you complete your pilgrimage, so it is very important to preserve your memories of the retreat as you connect them to the subsequent changes in your spiritual life. This journal should include reflections on each of your prayer periods, especially the review sessions, and any special prayers or insights that seem significant "in the moment". You also should collect any artwork you create during the retreat (e.g., poetry, drawings, etc.). Like your journey through the retreat, this journal should be uniquely suited to your spiritual needs and personality.

It is important that you not use your journal while preparing your prayers. Instead, you should record your preparatory notes in a small workbook (or on separate pages collected in a folder). These notes will present your thoughts and desires as you approach different topics during the retreat, while your journal will record the effects of your conversations with God — which may change your perceptions of the various issues and concerns you initially bring to your prayer. Keeping these two records of your retreat distinct and separate from each other will help you better understand the inner dynamics of your experiences while traveling with Brendan and his companions.

Finally, after completing your retreat, take some time to consider the materials in the "Returning Home" section. You should consider the first two exercises in separate sessions that are half the length of time you committed to prayer periods during the retreat — perhaps sharing these reflections in a special with the other members of your group shortly after the retreat. Also, you should follow the suggestions in "Nurturing the Courage of Pilgrims" as the spiritual gifts of your retreat mature in the months after your retreat. You will develop a special relationship with Brendan and his companions during your spiritual journey with them, so taking time for these considerations will offer a special opportunity to clarify the unique gifts you receive during the retreat.

As you create a vessel for your journey with God — deciding how it will be built and whether it should be large enough for companions — you also should contemplate the patterns and rhythms of prayer that will propel you through this deeply personal and highly intense spiritual pilgrimage. You know that you will shape the vessel for your voyage from the time and space you dedicate to it, but you also need to recognize that your prayer and other spiritual activities form the riggings of that vessel. So, you should consider the mental and spiritual rigors of the voyage before you. While God certainly will nourish and sustain you, the prayer techniques used during your journey will require discipline and effort if they are to open you completely to God's presence in your life.

With a clear understanding of the length of the journey you want to make and of the vessel you will build to complete it, you now should prepare yourself to set out on your spiritual pilgrimage. This book will guide you on your voyage as well as provide the various provisions you will need for the journey you select. Ultimately, however, your truest guide and companion during this retreat will be the Spirit of God traveling with you during your pilgrimage. So, you should proceed with confidence, knowing that you are about to enter into a profound conversation with a loving and nurturing God. You will need to trust in that conversation, learning both to accept the care God will provide during your time together and to embrace the desires God evokes in you.

This is a moment for generosity as God invites you deeper into a dynamic, loving relationship. May you find joy in learning to rely on the Spirit of God to guide you in your life choices, and may that Spirit help you strive for the courage to allow God to change you during your shared pilgrimage with Brendan and his companions.

A Pilgrimage to the Land of the Saints

A self-guided retreat
based on the voyage of
Saint Brendan the Navigator

• To complete this retreat, you will need the readings and prayer services presented in *A Journey to the Land of the Saints*. Since the footnotes to the reflections on Brendan's voyage offer insights that may assist your prayer, it is recommended that you purchase the book. However, if you are making this retreat in conjunction with the sequence of prayer services, you may choose to speak with a coordinator about access to these resources.

• A link to the digital files designed to accompany this retreat may be found in the resources section at the end of this book. These include an online mini-course introducing the Ignatian prayers used in this retreat as well as a PDF follow-up booklet intended to help you reflect on the spiritual gifts you received during your journey with Brendan and his companions as well as the leadings you might experience after returning home.

During your spiritual pilgrimage, you should listen for the rhythms and patterns of prayer that will mark your journey. Most of these will emerge during the course of the retreat through your conversations with God, but some will be shaped by the design of the retreat and the patterns of prayer used in it.

Note: Before you consider the following suggestions regarding your prayer, you will find it helpful to review the resources section at the end of this book. These include the texts for the examens used during this retreat, rituals you might use to create a sacred space for your prayer, and discussions of the types of Ignatian prayer used during this retreat.

In a daily life retreat, you will pray the morning examen each day before going out into the world and the evening examen each night before going to bed. At an appointed time on each day of the week, you will use the following order for prayer:
• Day 1 — Preparation

- Day 2 — 1st meditation
- Day 3 — 2nd meditation
- Day 4 — 3rd meditation
- Day 5 — 4th meditation
- Day 6 — The Application of the Senses
- Day 7 — Review

In a secluded retreat, you begin you your day with the morning examen and the preparation of your prayer for the day. These two activities may be integrated or conducted separately. Then, it is suggested that you pray using the following daily order:

- Late morning — 1st meditation
- Midday/early afternoon — 2nd meditation
- Late afternoon — 3rd meditation
- Early evening — 4th meditation
- Late evening — The Application of the Senses

Before going to bed, at least half an hour after the application of the senses, you should review your prayer and conduct the evening examen. Again, these activities may be combined into one exercise if you wish.

Note: *To integrate the examens into your preparation for each day or week (as well as the review at the end of these days or weeks), complete the exercises as they are explained in each section of the retreat and then replace the long prayers at the end of these reflections with the appropriate examen.*

With these schedules and concerns in mind, it would be helpful to reflect on the following issues before beginning a retreat:

Selecting a Bible Translation

You should decide which translation of the Bible will best help you hear God's voice during your prayers. It is important to remember that you will be using the Bible for prayer, not as an aid for your study of the biblical selections in the retreat. So, you may choose to use a different Bible than the one you regularly consult in your daily life.

Also, both the Ignatian and the Celtic spiritual traditions believe in an intimate relationship between Christ and his disciples that balances familiarity with deference. So, you will be asked during the retreat to speak with Jesus in a conversational tone similar to how you speak to your closest friends. Using a more contemporary translation of the Bible would help ease any discomfort you might feel as you approach Jesus in this way.

Pacing your Prayer

Whether in seclusion or in daily life, it is essential that you be consistent in the moments of your day devoted to prayer and reflection. You will be more likely to succeed if you remain mentally prepared for the spiritual and physical demands of the retreat and give them the energy and attention they require. Also, by faithfully honoring the times you designate for these spiritual activities, you will be able to relax and find pleasure in the rhythms of your retreat. Remember this time is an opportunity for you to have an extended conversation with a loving God. Feeling the familiarity created by the repeating patterns of the retreat will enhance this conversation as you become more comfortable in your prayer.

Also, it is important to remain faithful to the amount of time you commit to your prayer. You may be tempted to shorten a prayer period when you feel distracted, only to find that God breaks through your distraction. Or you may feel tempted to lengthen a powerful contemplation, only to find your thoughts diverted away from God. This retreat will be a very delicate time, so you need to be careful not to disrupt your emotional or spiritual equilibrium through erratic behavior. These suggestions are particularly important in the daily life retreat, where you have a very specific amount of time with God each day. But, during a secluded retreat, when your prayer permeates your entire day, you may be more flexible — allowing yourself to follow these leadings informally between prayer periods.

Note: It is important that you do not allow yourself to become too tired to remain faithful in your prayer while in seclusion. So, if you find this happening, you should eliminate one of the repetitions in your daily order until you feel called by God to pray all five suggested meditations.

Adapting the Instructions for Prayer

The instructions for this retreat cultivate habits of prayer by delineating clear structures for the different prayer exercises and employing consistent language when guiding each type of prayer presented in the retreat. The various movements within a particular time of prayer are marked by numbers [surrounded by brackets] and the phrasing for each type of exercise uses the same language — with variations for the content of the readings and the spiritual gifts desired in each meditation. In this way, you will become more confident in using different styles of prayer as the retreat progresses.

With time and practice, and as your confidence in using these prayer techniques grows, you may want to revise the particular activities within a prayer exercise to better suit your own personality. If so, it would be best if you begin by adapting the instructions used to set the scene for your imaginative prayer before changing any of the other sections. Also, you should not alter more than one bracketed section in the instructions at a time. In this way, you will be able to return easily to these instructions if you find that your adaptations disrupt your prayer.

However, if you choose to amend these instructions, it remains very important that you not change the particular movements of prayer delineated by the bracketed numbers. These stages within each prayer exercise shape the rhythm of your prayer, fostering spiritual habits that encourage an open disposition toward God and his desires.

Preparing for your Prayer

The time you spend preparing for prayer during your retreat, whether in daily life or in seclusion, should occur after you attend or read the prayer services. While vital to the successful completion of your retreat, the preparation of your prayer should never become a chore. Instead, it should be a relaxed and pleasant time of listening for God's voice in the readings that will shape the coming day or week of prayer (depending on whether you are making your retreat in daily life or in seclusion).

Participating in the prayer services during your retreat provides an opportunity for you to encounter the material for your subsequent prayer without overthinking it. So, if you are not attending the prayer services, you will need to consider ways to prayerfully engage the service that corresponds to the day or week of your retreat (including the excerpts from *The Voyage of Saint Brendan* and their companion meditations) — being careful to avoid a critical assessment of these materials so they may affect you emotionally. This will allow you to maintain a contemplative disposition as you prepare for your prayer during the retreat.

Note: If possible, you also should review the footnotes in the meditations on The Voyage of Saint Brendan *since their discussion of the affinities between Celtic and Ignatian spiritual ideals may help guide your prayers. Again, try to avoid overthinking these ideas by approaching them prayerfully and allowing them to evoke emotional responses in you.*

The main focus of your formal preparation time at the beginning of each day or week of the retreat should be the final section, where you express your desires and needs to God. These petitionary prayers will open your mind and your heart to hear what God has to say to you through the readings when you pray with them later. The rhythms — and, occasionally, specific words — of these prayers at the end of your preparation time need to be remembered so they may shape the beginning of each prayer period during the following day or week.

Repeating Seminal Prayers
During the course of your retreat, you will be asked to repeat and extend earlier meditations. The purpose of these repetitions is twofold: they help you deepen in your appreciation of the material at the heart of your prayer and they help you understand yourself as you respond to God through your prayers. Repetition will allow you to discern those aspects of your life where you are most receptive to God as well as where you resist God's presence.

So, it is important that you treat each moment of prayer as a new experience of God. Try to allow each time of prayer to remain unique, even as you return to a familiar reading. With time and effort, you will find that you are able to enter into your conversation with God more quickly and express yourself more comfortably.

Reviewing your Prayer
Learning to listen to God requires a willingness to assess honestly our disposition during our prayers and in our lives. By reviewing the prayers of your day or week, you learn as much about yourself as you do about the scriptures with which you pray. So, as you take time to review your prayer, allow space in your thoughts and feelings for God to speak to you about the gifts you have received and the graces that you still need.

Ultimately, the review periods in your retreat are not about thought. They serve as another opportunity for prayer in which your consciousness of God's presence in your life takes tangible shape.

While you certainly will remember seminal moments from the retreat long after it is finished, the deeper currents of God's activity during your prayer will become most evident through your careful consideration of the details of each moment you spend with God during the retreat.

Scheduling the Prayer Services

Note: These considerations are necessary only if you conduct the prayer services during a secluded retreat with companions. If you attend the prayer services while making your retreat in daily life, the rhythm of your prayer is coordinated to the prayer services (including the reflective service at the end of the sequence).

The prayer services present a clear boundary between the days of the retreat and provide one of the few shared events for a group making a secluded retreat together. So, it is very important to consider the time of day that best suits the spiritual desires and temperaments of the members of your group. With this in mind, it is recommended — but not required — that the prayer services be conducted as a morning prayer that introduces the readings and issues of the coming day.

This rhythm will sustain your group in prayer throughout the retreat. But you will need to decide when to conduct the final prayer service, which marks the end of your seclusion by summarizing your experiences and commissioning you back into the world.

The scheduling of this final prayer service will depend on the amount of time you commit to your retreat. It is recommended that you conduct the service on the tenth day of seclusion. However, you may need to end your retreat on the ninth day. If this is the case, you will need to remove some prayer periods from the retreat — the application of the senses, followed (if necessary) by the repetitions — depending on the time of day you intend to conduct the final prayer service at the conclusion of your retreat.

I • BARRIND'S STORY

Preparation

<u>Consideration of the Readings:</u>

After attending or prayerfully reading the prayer service for this day or week:

• Read (or hear) "Barrind's Story" and its companion reflection, "Walking with the Celtic Saints". Allow yourself to linger on any thoughts or phrases that seem particularly meaningful or relevant to your life. Then, record these moments in your workbook.

• Read Psalm 19 and John 1: 1-18. Again, pay careful attention to any phrases or images that seem particularly meaningful to you. Then, record these highlights from the psalm or Saint John's prologue in your workbook so you will remember them during the meditations on these readings in this section of the retreat.

• Read the story of Jesus with the Samaritan woman in John 4: 3-26. Make a mental note of each person's appearance and actions during the episode as well as the key elements of the story, including the setting. Again, consider any aspects of this story that speak strongly to you before recording these observations in your workbook.

<u>Note:</u> *You also should take a moment to consider any aspect of the prayer service from this day or week that seemed particularly significant to you.*

<u>Contemplation of Your Needs:</u>

When you are ready, concentrating on your breath or an object near you, allow any distractions to fade from your consciousness as you become aware of your desire to live in God's goodness. Feel yourself yearning to properly use the many gifts God has given you, to experience God's continuing care, and to be open to the immense love God shows for you.

Then, pray for your desires in the coming day or week. Ask that the divine presence all around you may be revealed, so you will have the courage to respond to anything God might ask you to do. Allow these desires to linger on your mind and in your heart for a few moments before slowly reviewing your notes on the readings for the coming day or week, asking God to be with you during these prayers — giving you the spiritual gifts you need from each of these readings as well as in your life after the retreat.

Finally, put your notes aside. Without straining your memory, consider in turn each of the readings for the coming day or week and allow them to take shape in your imagination — even if all you remember are small fragments. Prayerfully ponder how each reading affects you emotionally without overtly thinking about their content, asking God to illuminate the spiritual gifts offered in each reading — quieting your mind and creating a receptive space in yourself to see or hear the response.

Then, conclude by allowing these desires to fade from your consciousness as you offer this traditional prayer from Alexander Carmichael's *Carmina Gadelica*:

> *Bless to me, O God,*
> > *Each thing my eyes see;*
> *Bless to me, O God,*
> > *Each sound my ears hear;*
> *Bless to me, O God,*
> > *Each odor that goes to my nostrils;*
> *Bless to me, O God,*
> > *Each taste that goes to my lips;*
> > *Each note that goes to my song,*
> > *Each ray that guides my way,*
> > *Each thing that I pursue,*
> > *Each lure that tempts my will,*
> > *The zeal that seeks my living soul,*
> *The Three that seek my heart,*
> > *The zeal that seeks my living soul,*
> *The Three that seek my heart. Amen.*

Allow these words to linger on your mind and in your heart for a few moments and then, while they are still fresh in your memory, write the most important thoughts and feelings from this preparatory prayer in your workbook or journal.

Note: Remember the dynamics of this final section of your preparation, noting the way it unfolded as well as any specific phrases or images that shaped it. Allow these elements to guide you into the later prayers in this section of your retreat.

Verses 1 through 9

[1]   Become aware of your desire to live in God's goodness so you may use the many gifts God has given you. Feel God's continuing care for you and open yourself to the immense love God shows for you. Then, ask that the divine presence all around you may be revealed, so you will have the courage to respond to anything God might ask you to do.

As these desires fill your consciousness, allow all other concerns to fall aside as you focus on this specific time and place.

[2]   Then, when you are ready, in your imagination, see Saint Brendan welcome Barrind and listen to his story.

• Watch Barrind as he approaches Saint Brendan's abbey, noting his age as well as his physical characteristics and mannerisms. Look at what he is wearing, observing whether his clothing is clean or dirty as well as if he is carrying anything. Notice how he walks — and whether he seems tired or refreshed — as the monks welcome him and take him into a room to meet the abbot.

• Take a moment to look around the room, paying attention to its physical characteristics — its size and shape as well as the location of its doors and windows. See the furniture and decorations in the room, noting the shape and construction of these objects as well as their location. Look at the light sources, noting where they are located and whether the lighting is bright or muted. Notice whether the room feels humid or dry as well as whether it feels warm or cool on your skin.

• See and hear the monks who accompany Barrind to meet Brendan, noting the size of the group and their actions as they approach the abbot. Look at Brendan, noticing his physical characteristics and what he is doing as Barrind and the other monks enter the room. Observe the reactions of Brendan and Barrind as they first see one another, noting any differences between them and the other monks in terms of appearance or demeanor.

• See and hear Brendan as he welcomes Barrind, noticing the emotions displayed by each toward the other. Listen to them as they speak to one another, hearing Brendan invite his guest to tell the community about his journey. Observe the reaction of the monks to this invitation, noting what Brendan and Barrind are doing as the monks

20

prepare to hear Barrind's story.

• As you watch and listen to Barrind telling his story, focus your attention on Brendan. See where he is sitting, noting his physical appearance and his emotional demeanor as he listens to the story of the Land of the Saints. Take a moment to notice how Brendan behaves after hearing the story, observing how his response compares or contrasts with the other monks in his community.

[3]   As you hear Brendan invite his companions to pray in gratitude for this story, ask God to help you share in their prayer — either joining them as they pray or listening quietly to them.

Then, slowly read Psalm 19: 1-9 while seeing and hearing Brendan and his companions chant the psalm in your imagination. You may find that particular phrases touch you more deeply than others. Or you may find specific images, memories and emotions — perhaps even sounds and fragrances — associated with the different parts of the psalm. Make a mental note of these things.

After the monks conclude their prayer, allow their image to fade from your imagination as you become aware of the particular phrases and images from the psalm which touched you most deeply. Recall the emotions and memories — as well as any sounds or smells — evoked by the words of the psalm. Allow these key aspects of your prayer to linger on your mind and in your heart, making a mental note of any special feelings evoked by them.

When you are ready, speak with God in an open and informal manner about how the psalm expresses your own needs or desires — giving space for God to respond or to highlight different aspects of the psalm. Gradually allow your thoughts to recede as you focus on God's presence in your life and in the world around you.

[4]   When you are ready, take a moment to gather any important thoughts, emotions and memories from this meditation before concluding with this prayer from Alexander Carmichael's *Carmina Gadelica*:

O God of life, darken not to me your light,
O God of life, close not to me your joy,
O God of life, shut not to me your door,
      O God of life, refuse not to me your mercy,
      O God of life, quench toward me your wrath,
         O God of life, crown me with your gladness,
O God of life, crown me with your gladness. Amen.

[5]   After finishing your prayer, take 10-15 minutes in a quiet space

to reflect on the most significant moments from this time of prayer. Then, record your reflections in your journal.

Verses 1 through 14

[1]   Again, feel your desire to live in God's goodness so you may use the many gifts God has given you. Feeling God's continuing care to you, open yourself to the immense love God shows for you. Then, ask that the divine presence all around you may be revealed, so you will have the courage to respond to anything God might ask you to do.

As these desires fill your consciousness, allow all other concerns to fall aside as you focus on this specific time and place.

[2]   Then, when you are ready, in your imagination, see Saint Brendan welcome Barrind and listen to his story.

• Watch Barrind as he approaches Saint Brendan's abbey, noting his age as well as his physical characteristics and mannerisms. Look at what he is wearing, observing whether his clothing is clean or dirty as well as if he is carrying anything. Notice how he walks — and whether he seems tired or refreshed — as the monks welcome him and take him into a room to meet the abbot.

• Take a moment to look around the room, paying attention to its physical characteristics — its size and shape as well as the location of its doors and windows. See the furniture and decorations in the room, noting the shape and construction of these objects as well as their location. Look at the light sources, noting where they are located and whether the lighting is bright or muted. Notice whether the room feels humid or dry as well as whether it feels warm or cool on your skin.

• See and hear the monks who accompany Barrind to meet Brendan, noting the size of the group and their actions as they approach the abbot. Look at Brendan, noticing his physical characteristics and what he is doing as Barrind and the other monks enter the room. Observe the reactions of Brendan and Barrind as they first see one another, noting any differences between them and the other monks in terms of appearance or demeanor.

• See and hear Brendan as he welcomes Barrind, noticing the emotions displayed by each toward the other. Listen to them as they speak to one another, hearing Brendan invite his guest to tell the community about his journey. Observe the reaction of the monks to this invitation, noting what Brendan and Barrind are doing as the monks prepare to hear Barrind's story.

• As you watch and listen to Barrind telling his story, focus your attention on Brendan. See where he is sitting, noting his physical appearance and his emotional demeanor as he listens to the story of the Land of the Saints. Take a moment to notice how Brendan behaves after hearing the story, observing how his response compares or contrasts with the other monks in his community.

[3]   As you hear Brendan invite his companions to pray in gratitude for this story, ask God to help you share in their prayer — either joining them as they pray or listening quietly to them.

Then, slowly read Psalm 19: 1-14 while you imagine Brendan and his companions chanting the psalm. You may find that particular phrases touch you more deeply than others. Or you may find specific images, memories and emotions — perhaps even sounds and fragrances — associated with the different parts of the psalm. Make a mental note of these things.

After the monks conclude their prayer, allow their image to fade from your imagination as you become aware of the particular phrases and images from the psalm which touched you most deeply. Recall the emotions and memories — as well as any sounds or smells — evoked by the words of the psalm. Allow these key aspects of your prayer to linger on your mind and in your heart, making a mental note of any special feelings evoked by them.

When you are ready, speak with God in an open and informal manner about how the psalm expresses your own needs or desires — giving space for God to respond or to highlight different aspects of the psalm. Gradually allow your thoughts to recede as you focus on God's presence in your life and in the world around you.

[4]   When you are ready, take a moment to gather any important thoughts, emotions and memories from this meditation before concluding with this prayer:

O God of life, darken not to me your light,
O God of life, close not to me your joy,
O God of life, shut not to me your door,
    O God of life, refuse not to me your mercy,
    O God of life, quench toward me your wrath,
    O God of life, crown me with your gladness,
O God of life, crown me with your gladness. Amen.

[5]   Again, take 10-15 minutes in a quiet space to reflect on the most significant moments from this time of prayer. Then, record your reflections in your journal.

A consideration of John 1

Verses 1 through 18

[1]   Again, feel your desire to live in God's goodness so you may use the many gifts God has given you. Feeling God's continuing care to you, open yourself to the immense love God shows for you. Then, ask that the divine presence all around you may be revealed, so you will have the courage to respond to anything God might ask you to do.

As these desires fill your consciousness, allow all other concerns to fall aside as you focus on this specific time and place.

[2]   Then, when you are ready, in your imagination, listen with the monks of Saint Brendan's abbey to a reading of the prologue of Saint John's Gospel.

• Watch Brendan, Barrind and a group of monks as they enter the chapel, noting any physical or emotional differences between the various monks. Look in turn at each monk, observing what they are wearing or carrying as they enter the chapel. Notice where Brendan and Barrind sit in relation to the other monks.

• Take a moment to look around the chapel, paying attention to its physical characteristics — its size and shape as well as the height of its ceiling. See the altar, the pulpit (or lectern) and the seating for the monks, noting the shape and construction of these objects as well as their location. Look at the windows in the chapel, observing their physical appearance and how much light they provide. Notice whether the chapel feels humid or dry as well as whether it feels warm or cool on your skin.

• See and hear Brendan, Barrind and the other monks as they take their seats, noting the particular rituals or mannerisms of each monk. Look at Brendan as he sits down, noticing any differences between him and the other monks. Observe how Brendan interacts with the monks, noting the ways that the community responds to their abbot's actions.

• See and hear Brendan invite Barrind to present the gospel reading, noticing the responses both of Barrind and of the members of Brendan's community. Look at Brendan as he prepares to hear the gospel reading, seeing the ways that he enters into prayer. Observe Barrind's appearance and mannerisms as he approaches the pulpit or lectern, noting his emotional disposition as he opens the Gospel book.

[3]   As you prepare to hear the Gospel with Brendan and his

companions, ask God to guide your imagination into this reading. Take a moment to remain in this moment, feeling a sense of gentle expectancy.

Then, read John 1: 1-18 while you imagine Barrind proclaiming the prologue to Saint John's Gospel to the other monks. Note the tone of his voice and the rhythms of his speech as well as the words he accentuates. Linger on any phrases from the reading that touch you most deeply. Again, you may find specific images, memories and emotions — perhaps even sounds and fragrances — associated with the different parts of the reading and want to pay special attention to these things.

After Barrind concludes the reading and closes the Gospel book, allow his image to fade from your imagination as you recall the emotions and memories — as well as any sounds or smells — evoked by the reading. Allow these key aspects of your prayer to linger on your mind and in your heart for a moment.

[4]	Then, see Jesus standing or sitting in front of you. Look at him — noting his physical characteristics and demeanor — as you become aware of your feelings as you are with him. Remember that Jesus wants to reveal himself to you, so try to be aware of his feelings as he is with you. Consider what you need to say to him about your recent prayer and open yourself to hear what he needs to say to you.

When you are ready, speak with Jesus as you would a close friend in an informal conversation. Allow your imagination to guide you freely as you speak, remaining open to changes in the topics of conversation and giving Jesus the space to introduce the issues and concerns from your recent prayer that he thinks are important for you to hear.

[5]	When you are ready, take a moment to gather any important thoughts, emotions and memories from this meditation before concluding with this prayer:

> O God of life, darken not to me your light,
> O God of life, close not to me your joy,
> O God of life, shut not to me your door,
> > O God of life, refuse not to me your mercy,
> > O God of life, quench toward me your wrath,
> > O God of life, crown me with your gladness,
> O God of life, crown me with your gladness. Amen.

[6]	Again, take 10-15 minutes in a quiet space to reflect on the most significant moments from this time of prayer. Then, record your

reflections in your journal.

A Contemplation of John 4

Verses 3 through 26

[1]   Again, feel your desire to live in God's goodness so you may use the many gifts God has given you. Feeling God's continuing care to you, open yourself to the immense love God shows for you. Then, ask for the confidence to approach God with openness and trust, without being intimidated by the knowledge God has of every aspect of your existence — including your deepest insecurities and needs. Finally, pray that you will recognize and cherish the companions that God provides to help you on your journey through life.

As these desires fill your consciousness, allow all other concerns to fall aside as you focus on this specific time and place.

[2]   Then, when you are ready, slowly read the account of Jesus speaking with the Samaritan woman in John 4: 3-26. As you read, you may find particular phrases from the passage touching you more deeply than others and want to concentrate on these for a while. Or you may find yourself focusing on images, memories and emotions — perhaps even sounds and fragrances — associated with the different parts of the reading.

Linger on any phrases or moments from the reading that touched you deeply, noticing the feelings evoked by them.

[3]   Now, ask God to guide you into this event in your imagination. Allow God to provide the words and actions that help place you in this moment with Jesus — whether becoming a part of the story or observing it. While you may refer to the biblical account during your prayer, do not be afraid if your imagination leads Jesus or the Samaritan woman to expand their conversation during your prayer — adding different words or phrases, perhaps mirroring your own speech patterns.

• Watch Jesus as he approaches the well, noting his physical characteristics as well as his general demeanor. Look at the clothes he is wearing, observing if he brought anything with him. Notice how he walks and whether he seems tired or refreshed.

• Take a moment to look at the well, paying attention to its size and physical characteristics as well as the area around it. See the road it is on, noting any vegetation or animals around the well. Look at the sky and become aware of whether the day is sunny or cloudy, observing whether the air feels humid or dry. Notice whether you feel heat or wind on your skin as well as whether you feel warm or cool.

• See and hear the Samaritan woman as she approaches the well, noting her physical characteristics and mannerisms as well as her reaction to Jesus' presence. Look at the clothes she is wearing, noticing whether they are frayed or well-maintained. Observe the container she brought to the well, noting its size and construction as well as if she struggles to carry it.

• See and hear Jesus as he speaks with the Samaritan woman, noticing how the attitudes of each toward the other change while they speak. Listen to their conversation, watching the physical mannerisms of both Jesus and the Samaritan woman. Observe which parts of the conversation are most important to each person, noting the emotional reactions of Jesus and the Samaritan woman as they listen to each other.

When their conversation ends, allow these images to fade from your imagination. Become aware of the emotions and memories that touched you most deeply — phrases or images, sounds or smells, etc. Make a mental note of any strong feelings evoked by these aspects of your prayer.

[4]   Then, see Jesus standing or sitting in front of you. Look at him — noting his physical characteristics and demeanor — as you become aware of your feelings as you are with him. Remember that Jesus wants to reveal himself to you, so try to be aware of his feelings toward you. Consider what you need to say to him about your recent prayer and open yourself to hear what he needs to say to you.

When you are ready, speak with Jesus as you would a close friend in an informal conversation. Allow your imagination to guide you freely as you speak, remaining open to changes in the topics of conversation and giving Jesus the space to introduce the issues and concerns from your recent prayer that he thinks are important for you to hear.

[5]   When you are ready, take a moment to gather any important thoughts, emotions and memories from this contemplation before concluding with this prayer from Alexander Carmichael's *Carmina Gadelica*:

> *O God of life, darken not to me your light,*
> *O God of life, close not to me your joy,*
> *O God of life, shut not to me your door,*
> > *O God of life, refuse not to me your mercy,*
> > *O God of life, quench toward me your wrath,*
> > *O God of life, crown me with your gladness,*

O God of life, crown me with your gladness. Amen.

[6]   Again, take 10-15 minutes in a quiet space to reflect on the most significant moments from this time of prayer. Then, record your reflections in your journal.

An Application of the Senses

[1]   Again, feel your desire to live in God's goodness so you may use the many gifts God has given you. Feel God's continuing care as you open yourself to the immense love God shows for you — asking for the confidence to approach God with openness and trust, without being intimidated by the knowledge God has of every aspect of your existence. Remember also your desire to recognize and cherish the companions that God provides to help you on your journey through life.

Then, focus on this moment as all other concerns fade away.

[2]   When you are ready, in your imagination, recall the story of Barrind visiting Saint Brendan at his abbey. Allow the images and words of this story to linger and then slowly fade from your consciousness. Consider the images and feelings evoked in you during your prayer, feeling God's presence in these memories and becoming aware of the specific sensations associated with each image.

Then, in turn, remember your recent prayers on Psalm 19, the prologue to John's Gospel and Jesus with the Samaritan woman. As these prayers enter your memory, make a mental note of which senses are most active. You may see an image or a color, hear a sound or a phrase, or smell a scent or a fragrance. You may even taste a flavor or feel a sensation on your skin.

Finally, relax and allow these various memories and experiences to quietly enter and leave your consciousness without being controlled — whether they are clear or diffuse, whether they come quickly or slowly. Linger on the sensory images and memories being evoked in you — noticing any images or colors, any sounds or phrases, any scents or fragrances, any flavors or physical sensations associated with each prayer.

[3]   When you are ready, become completely still and clear your mind of all thoughts and concerns. Watch as God forms a small image or object in your mind containing the most important gift you have been given during this particular time of prayer — the thought or awareness that you most need to carry with you into your life.

Reverently pick up the object or image, looking at it carefully and becoming aware of the divine presence contained within it. Take a moment to register what it looks like and how it feels in your hand. Then, feel the joy and confidence that comes from touching the

31

presence of God as you accept this gift, offering a short prayer of gratitude while you relax into the pleasure of this moment.

[4]   Then, conclude by offering this prayer:

O God of life, darken not to me your light,
O God of life, close not to me your joy,
O God of life, shut not to me your door,
  O God of life, refuse not to me your mercy,
  O God of life, quench toward me your wrath,
  O God of life, crown me with your gladness,
O God of life, crown me with your gladness. Amen.

[5]   While your experiences are still fresh in your mind, record the most significant impressions or sensations from this time of prayer in your journal and thank God for the special gift you received from him.

Review

[1]   Remember your desire to be aware of God's presence in everything around you. Recall how you asked for the courage to respond fully to anything God might ask you to do. Then, take a moment to allow the words, thoughts and feelings from your prayers during the last day or week to linger — on your mind and in your heart — before asking God to reveal His presence in these various memories.

[2]   Think about the story of Barrind visiting Saint Brendan at his abbey. Remember the parts of the story that spoke most powerfully to you and think about how elements of this story resurfaced in your recent prayers on Psalm 139 and Jesus with the Samaritan woman. Ask God to help you understand these moments.

[3]   Consider your meditations on Psalm 19. Recall the most powerful images, phrases or feelings from your prayer. Ask yourself what gifts God gave to you through these moments, perhaps offering you new insights or perhaps affirming an important aspect of your faith. Ask yourself how God may be calling you to change through these moments, being as specific as possible.

Examine your disposition as you prayed, noting whether prayer came easily or with resistance. Recall the easiest moments in your prayer and any moments of joy you may have experienced. Remember also if you encountered any difficulty opening yourself to God or if you felt any sadness as you prayed. Ask God to help you understand why these feelings surfaced.

Bring to mind any moments when you added personal elements — familiar places or people from your life — or connected your prayers to other scriptures or spiritual writings. Ask yourself how these additions helped or hindered you as you prayed. Again, if you do not know why this happened, ask God to help you understand.

[4]   Ponder your meditation on Saint John's prologue. Then, review your prayer in the same way as your earlier reflection on Psalm 19.

[5]   Review your contemplation of Jesus at the well with the Samaritan woman, allowing a mental picture of this event to form in your mind as you recall the perspective from which you experienced this conversation. Then, ponder your prayer in the same way as your earlier reflections on Psalm 19 and Saint John's prologue.

[5]   Recall the ebb and flow of sensory impressions and feelings that marked your application of the senses. Isolate the most memorable

moments and sensory impressions from your prayer and reflect on how God used these moments to give you a particular gift, perhaps offering you new insights or changing you in some way. Then, consider what you want to offer God in return for these moments.

[6]   Finally, remember the times when images or feelings from the readings of this day or week surfaced outside these prayer periods. Consider those moments or events in which God's presence or guidance was especially strong as well as any moments when you were struggling. Think about the most memorable aspects of these experiences, asking God to explain their significance.

[7]   Take a moment to allow the words, thoughts and feelings of these prayers to linger on your mind and in your heart. Then, conclude by asking for God's continued presence and guidance as you offer this prayer from Alexander Carmichael's *Carmina Gadelica*:

> Bless to me, O God,
>   Each thing my eyes see;
> Bless to me, O God,
>   Each sound my ears hear;
> Bless to me, O God,
>   Each odor that goes to my nostrils;
> Bless to me, O God,
>   Each taste that goes to my lips;
>   Each note that goes to my song,
>   Each ray that guides my way,
>   Each thing that I pursue,
>   Each lure that tempts my will,
>   The zeal that seeks my living soul,
> The Three that seek my heart,
>   The zeal that seeks my living soul,
> The Three that seek my heart. Amen.

[8]   After finishing these prayers, summarize your reflections on the gifts or graces you received during the prayers of this last day or week and record these insights in your journal. Also, remember to include any insights or desires that came to you between prayer periods. Then, being as specific as possible, you should conclude this summary with a short prayer of gratitude for God's generosity toward you during the previous day or week.

II • THE BROTHERS VISIT HOLY ENDA
& AN UNINHABITED HOUSE

Preparation

Consideration of the Readings:
     After attending or prayerfully reading the prayer service for this day or week:
     • Read (or hear) "The Brothers Visit Holy Enda & An Uninhabited House" and its companion reflection, "Finding Christ in All Things". Allow yourself to linger on any thoughts or phrases that seem particularly meaningful or relevant to your life. Then, record these moments in your workbook.
     • Read Psalm 139. Again, pay careful attention to any phrases or images that seem particularly meaningful to you. Then, record these highlights from the psalm in your workbook so you will remember them during the meditations on these readings in this section of the retreat.
     • Read about Jesus' call of the first disciples in John 1: 35-51. Make a mental note of each person's appearance and actions during the episode as well as the key elements of the story, including the setting. Again, consider any aspects of this story that speak strongly to you before recording these observations in your workbook.

     Note: You also should take a moment to consider any aspect of the prayer service from this day or week that seemed particularly significant to you.

Contemplation of Your Needs:
     When you are ready, concentrating on your breath or an object near you, allow any distractions to fade from your consciousness as you become aware of your desire to live in God's goodness. Feel yourself yearning to properly use the many gifts God has given you, to experience God's continuing care, and to be open to the immense love God shows for you.
     Then, pray for your desires in the coming day or week. Ask for the confidence to approach God with openness and trust, without being intimidated by the knowledge God has of every aspect of your existence — including your deepest insecurities and needs. Also, pray that you will recognize and cherish the companions that God provides to help you on your journey through life. Allow these desires to linger

on your mind and in your heart for a few moments before slowly reviewing your notes on the readings for the coming day or week, asking God to be with you during these prayers — giving you the spiritual gifts you need from each of these readings as well as in your life after the retreat.

Finally, put your notes aside. Without straining your memory, consider in turn each of the readings for the coming day or week and allow them to take shape in your imagination — even if all you remember are small fragments. Prayerfully ponder how each reading affects you emotionally without overtly thinking about their content, asking God to illuminate the spiritual gifts offered in each reading — quieting your mind and creating a receptive space in yourself to see or hear the response.

Then, conclude by allowing these desires to fade from your consciousness as you offer this traditional prayer from Alexander Carmichael's *Carmina Gadelica*:

> *Bless to me, O God,*
>> *Each thing my eyes see;*
> *Bless to me, O God,*
>> *Each sound my ears hear;*
> *Bless to me, O God,*
>> *Each odor that goes to my nostrils;*
> *Bless to me, O God,*
>> *Each taste that goes to my lips;*
>> *Each note that goes to my song,*
>> *Each ray that guides my way,*
>> *Each thing that I pursue,*
>> *Each lure that tempts my will,*
>> *The zeal that seeks my living soul,*
> *The Three that seek my heart,*
>> *The zeal that seeks my living soul,*
> *The Three that seek my heart. Amen.*

Allow these words to linger on your mind and in your heart for a few moments and then, while they are still fresh in your memory, write the most important thoughts and feelings from this preparatory prayer in your workbook or journal.

Note: Remember to allow the dynamics of this preparation — the way it unfolded as well as any specific phrases or images that shaped it — to guide you into the later prayers in this section of your retreat.

Verses 1 through 12

[1]   Become aware of your desire to live in God's goodness so you may use the many gifts God has given you. Feel God's continuing care for you and open yourself to the immense love God shows for you. Then, ask for the confidence to approach God with openness and trust. Also, pray that you may recognize and cherish the companions that God provides to help you on your journey through life.

As these desires fill your consciousness, allow all other concerns to fall aside as you focus on this specific time and place.

[2]   Then, when you are ready, in your imagination, join Brendan and his companions in your imagination as they begin their journey.

• Watch Saint Enda as he blesses Brendan and his companions, noting his appearance and mannerisms as well as whether he is alone with his guests or accompanied by other members of his community. Look around his dwelling, observing it shape and size as well as any furniture or decorations in it. Notice how Brendan responds to receiving this blessing from Saint Enda — and if his response differs from the monks traveling with him.

• Take a moment to look at Brendan and his companions as they leave Enda and travel to a location near the coast, paying attention to the attitudes and activities of each monk during the journey. See the monks build a boat and gather provisions for their journey, noting the size of the boat and the various supplies being placed in it. Look at Saint Brendan as he and his companions work, observing his actions as well as his disposition toward his companions. Notice the physical actions — and emotional state — of each monk as the time to leave draws closer.

• See and hear Brendan and his companions as they set to sea, noting the ways they work together and the tone of their conversation. Look at them while they are on the ocean, noticing how they respond when catching favorable winds in their sail or when needing to row through heavy waves. Observe the differences between Brendan and his companions during these moments, noting the different ways Brendan responds to the actions and attitudes of his monks.

• See and hear Brendan and his companions as they come upon land for the first time, noting the appearance of the shoreline and the land beyond it. Listen to the monks while they land their vessel, hearing

Brendan as he guides the monks and how they respond to their abbot. Observe a dog as it approaches the monks after they land and leads them to a great hall, noting its appearance and manner as it guides Brendan — as well as the reactions of Brendan and his companions as they enter the great hall.

• As Brendan and the monks prepare for their meal, focus your attention on Brendan. See where he is sitting and how he speaks to the various monks, noting his appearance and demeanor as the food is presented to the monks. Take a moment to look around the great hall — noting its size and shape as well as the furniture, tableware and decorations in it — while observing how Brendan's response to the gift of this food and shelter differs from the other monks in his company.

[3]   Listen to Brendan as he invites his companions to express their gratitude in prayer and ask God to help you to share in that prayer — either joining them as they pray or listening quietly to them.

Then, slowly read Psalm 139: 1-12 while seeing and hearing Brendan and his companions chant the psalm in your imagination. You may find that particular phrases touch you more deeply than others. Or you may find specific images, memories and emotions — perhaps even sounds and fragrances — associated with the different parts of the psalm. Make a mental note of these things.

After the monks conclude their prayer, allow their image to fade from your imagination as you become aware of the particular phrases and images from the psalm which touched you most deeply. Recall the emotions and memories — as well as any sounds or smells — evoked by the words of the psalm. Allow these key aspects of your prayer to linger on your mind and in your heart, making a mental note of any special feelings evoked by them.

When you are ready, speak with God in an open and informal manner about how the psalm expresses your own needs or desires — giving space for God to respond or to highlight different aspects of the psalm. Gradually allow your thoughts to recede as you focus on God's presence in your life and in the world around you.

[4]   When you are ready, take a moment to gather any important thoughts, emotions and memories from this meditation before concluding with this prayer from Alexander Carmichael's *Carmina Gadelica*:

> *O God of life, darken not to me your light,*
> *O God of life, close not to me your joy,*
> *O God of life, shut not to me your door,*

O God of life, refuse not to me your mercy,
O God of life, quench toward me your wrath,
O God of life, crown me with your gladness,
O God of life, crown me with your gladness. Amen.

[5]   Take 5-10 minutes to reflect on the most significant moments from this time of prayer. Then, record your preliminary reflections in your journal.

A repeated meditation on Psalm 139

Verses 1 through 17, continuing with Verses 23 & 24

[1]   Again, feel your desire to live in God's goodness so you may use the many gifts God has given you. Feeling God's continuing care to you, open yourself to the immense love God shows for you. Then, ask for the confidence to approach God with openness and trust. Also, pray that you may recognize and cherish the companions that God provides to help you on your journey through life.

As these desires fill your consciousness, allow all other concerns to fall aside as you focus on this specific time and place.

[2]   Then, when you are ready, in your imagination, join Brendan and his companions in your imagination as they begin their journey.

• Watch Saint Enda as he blesses Brendan and his companions, noting his appearance and mannerisms as well as whether he is alone with his guests or accompanied by other members of his community. Look around his dwelling, observing it shape and size as well as any furniture or decorations in it. Notice how Brendan responds to receiving this blessing from Saint Enda — and if his response differs from the monks traveling with him.

• Take a moment to look at Brendan and his companions as they leave Enda and travel to a location near the coast, paying attention to the attitudes and activities of each monk during the journey. See the monks build a boat and gather provisions for their journey, noting the size of the boat and the various supplies being placed in it. Look at Saint Brendan as he and his companions work, observing his actions as well as his disposition toward his companions. Notice the physical actions — and emotional state — of each monk as the time to leave draws closer.

• See and hear Brendan and his companions as they set to sea, noting the ways they work together and the tone of their conversation. Look at them while they are on the ocean, noticing how they respond when catching favorable winds in their sail or when needing to row through heavy waves. Observe the differences between Brendan and his companions during these moments, noting the different ways Brendan responds to the actions and attitudes of his monks.

• See and hear Brendan and his companions as they come upon land for the first time, noting the appearance of the shoreline and the land beyond it. Listen to the monks while they land their vessel, hearing

Brendan as he guides the monks and how they respond to their abbot. Observe a dog as it approaches the monks after they land and leads them to a great hall, noting its appearance and manner as it guides Brendan — as well as the reactions of Brendan and his companions as they enter the great hall.

    • As Brendan and the monks prepare for their meal, focus your attention on Brendan. See where he is sitting and how he speaks to the various monks, noting his appearance and demeanor as the food is presented to the monks. Take a moment to look around the great hall — noting its size and shape as well as the furniture, tableware and decorations in it — while observing how Brendan's response to the gift of this food and shelter differs from the other monks in his company.

[3]   Listen to Brendan as he invites his companions to express their gratitude in prayer and ask God to help you to share in that prayer — either joining them as they pray or listening quietly to them.

    Then, slowly read Psalm 139: 1-17, 23-24 while you imagine Brendan and his companions chanting the psalm. You may find that particular phrases touch you more deeply than others. Or you may find specific images, memories and emotions — perhaps even sounds and fragrances — associated with the different parts of the psalm. Make a mental note of these things.

    After the monks conclude their prayer, allow their image to fade from your imagination as you become aware of the particular phrases and images from the psalm which touched you most deeply. Recall the emotions and memories — as well as any sounds or smells — evoked by the words of the psalm. Allow these key aspects of your prayer to linger on your mind and in your heart, making a mental note of any special feelings evoked by them.

    When you are ready, speak with God in an open and informal manner about how the psalm expresses your own needs or desires — giving space for God to respond or to highlight different aspects of the psalm. Gradually allow your thoughts to recede as you focus on God's presence in your life and in the world around you.

[4]   When you are ready, take a moment to gather any important thoughts, emotions and memories from this meditation before concluding with this prayer:

       O God of life, darken not to me your light,
       O God of life, close not to me your joy,
       O God of life, shut not to me your door,
           O God of life, refuse not to me your mercy,

O God of life, quench toward me your wrath,
O God of life, crown me with your gladness,
O God of life, crown me with your gladness. Amen.

[5]   Again, take 5-10 minutes to reflect on the most significant moments from this time of prayer. Then, record your preliminary reflections in your journal.

Verses 35 through 42

[1]   Again, feel your desire to live in God's goodness so you may use the many gifts God has given you. Feeling God's continuing care to you, open yourself to the immense love God shows for you. Then, ask for the confidence to approach God with openness and trust. Also, pray that you may recognize and cherish the companions that God provides to help you on your journey through life.

As these desires fill your consciousness, allow all other concerns to fall aside as you focus on this specific time and place.

[2]   Then, when you are ready, slowly read the account of Jesus calling his first disciples in John 1: 35-42. As you read, you may find particular phrases from the passage touching you more deeply than others and want to concentrate on these for a while. Or you may find yourself focusing on images, memories and emotions — perhaps even sounds and fragrances — associated with the different parts of the reading.

Linger on any phrases or moments from the reading that touched you deeply, noticing the feelings evoked by them.

[3]   Now, ask God to guide you into this event in your imagination. Allow God to provide the words and actions that help place you in this moment with Jesus — whether becoming a part of the story or observing it. While you may refer to the biblical account during your prayer, do not be afraid if your imagination leads Jesus, John the Baptist or the first disciples to expand their conversation during your prayer — adding different words or phrases, perhaps mirroring your own speech patterns.

• Watch John the Baptist as he speaks with his disciples, noting how John's different disciples respond when he points to Jesus. Look at John's disciples as they speak about Jesus, observing the different actions and attitudes within the group. Notice the emotional responses of John the Baptist and those around him as some of his disciples leave to follow Jesus.

• Take a moment to watch Jesus as he speaks to John's former disciples, paying attention to his mannerisms and tone of voice. Listen to Jesus as he speaks to the group on the way to his dwelling, noting the various reactions of different members of the group to what Jesus says to them. Look at where Jesus is staying, observing its physical characteristics as well as any furniture or decorations in it. Notice how Jesus speaks with John's former disciples as well as what he says and the ways he acts to offer hospitality to his guests.

• See and hear Andrew as he leaves to find his brother, noting the differences in their physical and emotional qualities. Listen to their conversation, noticing Andrew's enthusiasm and his insistence that Simon Peter come and meet Jesus. Observe Simon Peter's reaction to Andrew as he speaks about Jesus, noting how this changes during their conversation — and after he meets Jesus.

• See and hear Jesus ask Philip to follow him, noticing Philip's response and what he says when he finds Nathaniel. Listen to Philip and Nathaniel as they speak about Jesus, hearing the disdain in Nathaniel's voice as well as Philip's words as he implores Nathaniel to come with him to meet Jesus. Observe how Nathaniel's attitude changes as he speaks with Jesus, noting Jesus' behavior and demeanor as he speaks with Nathaniel.

When their conversation ends, allow these images to fade from your imagination. Become aware of the emotions and memories that touched you most deeply — phrases or images, sounds or smells, etc. Make a mental note of any strong feelings evoked by these aspects of your prayer.

[4]   Then, see Jesus standing or sitting in front of you. Look at him — noting his physical characteristics and demeanor — as you become aware of your feelings as you are with him. Remember that Jesus wants to reveal himself to you, so try to be aware of his feelings toward you. Consider what you need to say to him about your recent prayer and open yourself to hear what he needs to say to you.

When you are ready, speak with Jesus as you would a close friend in an informal conversation. Allow your imagination to guide you freely as you speak, remaining open to changes in the topics of conversation and giving Jesus the space to introduce the issues and concerns from your recent prayer that he thinks are important for you to hear.

[5]   When you are ready, take a moment to gather any important thoughts, emotions and memories from this contemplation before concluding with this prayer:

O God of life, darken not to me your light,
O God of life, close not to me your joy,
O God of life, shut not to me your door,
    O God of life, refuse not to me your mercy,

O God of life, quench toward me your wrath,
O God of life, crown me with your gladness,
O God of life, crown me with your gladness. Amen.

[6]   Again, take 5-10 minutes to reflect on the most significant moments from this time of prayer. Then, record your preliminary reflections in your journal.

A repeated contemplation of John 1

Verses 35 through 51

[1]   Again, feel your desire to live in God's goodness so you may use the many gifts God has given you. Feeling God's continuing care to you, open yourself to the immense love God shows for you. Then, ask for the confidence to approach God with openness and trust. Also, pray that you may recognize and cherish the companions that God provides to help you on your journey through life.

As these desires fill your consciousness, allow all other concerns to fall aside as you focus on this specific time and place.

[2]   Then, when you are ready, slowly read the account of Jesus calling his first disciples in John 1: 35-51. As you read, you may find particular phrases from the passage touching you more deeply than others and want to concentrate on these for a while. Or you may find yourself focusing on images, memories and emotions — perhaps even sounds and fragrances — associated with the different parts of the reading.

Linger on any phrases or moments from the reading that touched you deeply, noticing the feelings evoked by them.

[3]   Now, ask God to guide you into this event in your imagination. Allow God to provide the words and actions that help place you in this moment with Jesus — whether becoming a part of the story or observing it. While you may refer to the biblical account during your prayer, do not be afraid if your imagination leads Jesus, John the Baptist or the disciples to expand their conversation during your prayer — adding different words or phrases, perhaps mirroring your own speech patterns.

Note: *Allow your memories from your earlier contemplation of this episode to guide you back into the conversations between Jesus and his earliest disciples.*

• Watch John the Baptist as he speaks with his disciples, noting his physical characteristics and mannerisms as he sees Jesus. Look at Jesus as he passes the group, observing his appearance and demeanor as well as anything that distinguishes him from the other people. Notice how John's different disciples respond when he points to Jesus.

• Take a moment to look at the area around John the Baptist

and his disciples, paying attention to the people waiting to listen to John or to be baptized by him as well as what they are doing as John speaks to his disciples. See the river, noting its size and the topography of its bank as well as any vegetation or animals near it. Look at the sky and become aware of whether the day is sunny or cloudy, observing whether the air feels humid or dry. Notice whether you feel heat or wind on your skin as well as whether you feel warm or cool.

• See and hear the John's disciples as they speak about Jesus, noting the different actions and attitudes within the group. Listen as some disciples leave John to follow Jesus, hearing what they say to John and the other disciples before and as they depart and whether they run or walk to approach Jesus. Observe the emotional responses of John the Baptist and his remaining disciples as the group departs, noting any differences between John and his disciples.

• See and hear John's former disciples as Jesus as he turns to speak to them, noting his manner and tone of voice as he speaks. Listen to Jesus as he invites them to follow him and guides the group to his dwelling, making mental note about where Jesus is staying — whether in a house or an inn or outdoors — and noticing the various reactions of different members of the group to what Jesus says to them. Observe Andrew as he leaves to invite his brother to meet Jesus, noting Simon Peter's response to meeting Jesus.

When their conversation ends, allow these images to fade from your imagination. Become aware of the emotions and memories that touched you most deeply — phrases or images, sounds or smells, etc. Make a mental note of any strong feelings evoked by these aspects of your prayer.

[4]   Then, see Jesus standing or sitting in front of you. Look at him — noting his physical characteristics and demeanor — as you become aware of your feelings as you are with him. Remember that Jesus wants to reveal himself to you, so try to be aware of his feelings toward you. Consider what you need to say to him about your recent prayer and open yourself to hear what he needs to say to you.

When you are ready, speak with Jesus as you would a close friend in an informal conversation. Allow your imagination to guide you freely as you speak, remaining open to changes in the topics of conversation and giving Jesus the space to introduce the issues and concerns from your recent prayer that he thinks are important for you to hear.

[5]   When you are ready, take a moment to gather any important

thoughts, emotions and memories from this contemplation before concluding with this prayer:

> *O God of life, darken not to me your light,*
> *O God of life, close not to me your joy,*
> *O God of life, shut not to me your door,*
> > *O God of life, refuse not to me your mercy,*
> > *O God of life, quench toward me your wrath,*
> > *O God of life, crown me with your gladness,*
> *O God of life, crown me with your gladness. Amen.*

[6] Again, take 5-10 minutes to reflect on the most significant moments from this time of prayer. Then, record your preliminary reflections in your journal.

An Application of the Senses

[1]   Again, feel your desire to live in God's goodness so you may use the many gifts God has given you. Feel God's continuing care as you open yourself to the immense love God shows for you and ask for the confidence to approach God with openness and trust. Also, pray that you may recognize and cherish the companions that God provides to help you on your journey through life. Then, focus on this moment as all other concerns fade away.

[2]   When you are ready, in your imagination, call to mind the various events as Saint Brendan and his companions began their journey. Allow the images and words of this story to linger and then slowly fade from your consciousness. Consider the images and feelings evoked in you during your prayer, feeling God's presence in these memories and becoming aware of the specific sensations associated with each image.

Then, in turn, remember your recent prayers on Psalm 139 and Jesus with his earliest disciples. As these prayers enter your memory, make a mental note of which senses are most active. You may see an image or a color, hear a sound or a phrase, or smell a scent or a fragrance. You may even taste a flavor or feel a sensation on your skin.

Finally, relax and allow these various memories and experiences to quietly enter and leave your consciousness without being controlled — whether they are clear or diffuse, whether they come quickly or slowly. Linger on the sensory images and memories being evoked in you — noticing any images or colors, any sounds or phrases, any scents or fragrances, any flavors or physical sensations associated with each prayer.

[3]   When you are ready, become completely still and clear your mind of all thoughts and concerns. Watch as God forms a small image or object in your mind containing the most important gift you have been given during this particular time of prayer — the thought or awareness that you most need to carry with you into your life.

Reverently pick up the object or image, looking at it carefully and becoming aware of the divine presence contained within it. Take a moment to register what it looks like and how it feels in your hand. Then, feel the joy and confidence that comes from touching the presence of God as you accept this gift, offering a short prayer of gratitude while you relax into the pleasure of this moment.

[4]   Then, conclude by offering this prayer:
        O God of life, darken not to me your light,
        O God of life, close not to me your joy,
        O God of life, shut not to me your door,
                O God of life, refuse not to me your mercy,
                O God of life, quench toward me your wrath,
                O God of life, crown me with your gladness,
        O God of life, crown me with your gladness. Amen.
[5]   While your experiences are still fresh in your mind, record the most significant impressions or sensations from this time of prayer in your journal and thank God for the special gift you received from him.

Review

[1]   Remember your desire to approach God without being intimidated by the knowledge God has of every aspect of your existence, including your deepest insecurities and needs. Recall how you asked to recognize and cherish the companions that God provides to help you on your journey through life. Then, take a moment to allow the words, thoughts and feelings from your prayers during the last day or week to linger — on your mind and in your heart — before asking God to reveal His presence in these various memories.

[2]   Think about the events as Saint Brendan and his companions began their journey. Remember the parts of the story that spoke most powerfully to you and think about how elements of this story resurfaced in your recent prayers on Psalm 139 and Jesus with his first disciples. Ask God to help you understand these moments.

[3]   Consider your meditations on Psalm 139. Recall the most powerful images, phrases or feelings from your prayer. Ask yourself what gifts God gave to you through these moments, perhaps offering you new insights or perhaps affirming an important aspect of your faith. Ask yourself how God may be calling you to change through these moments, being as specific as possible.

Examine your disposition as you prayed, noting whether prayer came easily or with resistance. Recall the easiest moments in your prayer and any moments of joy you may have experienced. Remember also if you encountered any difficulty opening yourself to God or if you felt any sadness as you prayed. Ask God to help you understand why these feelings surfaced.

Bring to mind any moments when you added personal elements — familiar places or people from your life — or connected your prayers to other scriptures or spiritual writings. Ask yourself how these additions helped or hindered you as you prayed. Again, if you do not know why this happened, ask God to help you understand.

[4]   Ponder your contemplation of Jesus with the earliest disciples, allowing a mental picture of these events to form in your mind as you recall the perspective from which you experienced them. Then, review your prayer in the same way as your earlier reflection on Psalm 139.

[5]   Recall the ebb and flow of sensory impressions and feelings that marked your application of the senses. Isolate the most memorable moments and sensory impressions from your prayer and reflect on how

God used these moments to give you a particular gift, perhaps offering you new insights or changing you in some way. Then, consider what you want to offer God in return for these moments.

[6]   Finally, remember the times when images or feelings from the readings of this day or week surfaced outside these prayer periods. Consider those moments or events in which God's presence or guidance was especially strong as well as any moments when you were struggling. Think about the most memorable aspects of these experiences, asking God to explain their significance.

[7]   Take a moment to allow the words, thoughts and feelings of these prayers to linger on your mind and in your heart. Then, conclude by asking for God's continued presence and guidance as you offer this prayer:

> *Bless to me, O God,*
> > *Each thing my eyes see;*
> *Bless to me, O God,*
> > *Each sound my ears hear;*
> *Bless to me, O God,*
> > *Each odor that goes to my nostrils;*
> *Bless to me, O God,*
> > *Each taste that goes to my lips;*
> > *Each note that goes to my song,*
> > *Each ray that guides my way,*
> > *Each thing that I pursue,*
> > *Each lure that tempts my will,*
> > *The zeal that seeks my living soul,*
> *The Three that seek my heart,*
> > *The zeal that seeks my living soul,*
> *The Three that seek my heart. Amen.*

[8]   After finishing these prayers, summarize your reflections on the gifts or graces you received during the prayers of this last day or week and record these insights in your journal. Then, being as specific as possible, you should conclude this summary with a short prayer of gratitude for God's generosity toward you during the previous day or week.

III • THE ISLAND OF SHEEP
& THE LEVIATHAN JASCONIUS

Preparation

<u>Consideration of the Readings:</u>

After attending or prayerfully reading the prayer service for this day or week:

• Read (or hear) "The Island of Sheep & The Leviathan Jasconius" and its companion reflection, "Sharing in the Love of the Trinity". Allow yourself to linger on any thoughts or phrases that seem particularly meaningful or relevant to your life. Then, record these moments in your workbook.

• Read Psalms 27 and 62. Again, pay careful attention to any phrases or images that seem particularly meaningful to you. Then, record these highlights from the psalms in your workbook so you will remember them during the meditations on these readings in this section of the retreat.

• Read about Jesus at Cana in John 2: 1-11. Make a mental note of each person's appearance and actions during the episode as well as the key elements of the story, including the setting. Again, consider any aspects of this story that speak strongly to you before recording these observations in your workbook.

<u>Note:</u> You also should take a moment to consider any aspect of the prayer service from this day or week that seemed particularly significant to you.

<u>Contemplation of Your Needs:</u>

When you are ready, concentrating on your breath or an object near you, allow any distractions to fade from your consciousness as you become aware of your desire to live in God's goodness. Feel yourself yearning to properly use the many gifts God has given you, to experience God's continuing care, and to be open to the immense love God shows for you.

Then, pray for your desires in the coming day or week. Ask that you may be open to the divine presence all around you, helping you accept the many gifts that God gives you each day. Also, pray that you may trust in God's care and protection, giving you the courage to confront the many challenges you face in life. Allow these desires to linger on your mind and in your heart for a few moments before slowly reviewing your notes on the readings for the coming day or week, asking God to be with you during these prayers — giving you the spiritual gifts you need from each of these readings as well as in your life after the retreat.

Finally, put your notes aside. Without straining your memory, consider in turn each of the readings for the coming day or week and allow them to take shape in your imagination — even if all you remember are small fragments. Prayerfully ponder how each reading affects you emotionally without overtly thinking about their content, asking God to illuminate the spiritual gifts offered in each reading — quieting your mind and creating a receptive space in yourself to see or hear the response.

Then, conclude by allowing these desires to fade from your consciousness as you offer this traditional prayer from Alexander Carmichael's *Carmina Gadelica*:

> *Bless to me, O God,*
> > *Each thing my eyes see;*
> *Bless to me, O God,*
> > *Each sound my ears hear;*
> *Bless to me, O God,*
> > *Each odor that goes to my nostrils;*
> *Bless to me, O God,*
> > *Each taste that goes to my lips;*
> > *Each note that goes to my song,*
> > *Each ray that guides my way,*
> > *Each thing that I pursue,*
> > *Each lure that tempts my will,*
> > *The zeal that seeks my living soul,*
> > *The Three that seek my heart,*
> > *The zeal that seeks my living soul,*
> > *The Three that seek my heart. Amen.*

Allow these words to linger on your mind and in your heart for a few moments and then, while they are still fresh in your memory, write the most important thoughts and feelings from this preparatory prayer in your workbook or journal.

Note: Remember to allow the dynamics of this preparation — the way it unfolded as well as any specific phrases or images that shaped it — to guide you into the later prayers in this section of your retreat.

Verses 1 through 14

[1]   Become aware of your desire to live in God's goodness so you may use the many gifts God has given you. Feel God's continuing care for you and open yourself to the immense love God shows for you. Then, ask that you may be open to the divine presence all around you. Also, pray that you may trust in God's care and protection — giving you the courage to confront the many challenges you face in life.

As these desires fill your consciousness, allow all other concerns to fall aside as you focus on this specific time and place.

[2]   Then, when you are ready, travel in your imagination with Brendan and his companions as they leave the great hall and travel to the Island of Sheep.

• Watch Brendan and his fellow monks leave the great hall and return to their boat, noting the supplies and other items they take with them as they depart. Look at each monk as he places supplies into the boat, observing the different attitudes displayed by each — eagerness, hesitation, anxiety or excitement — as they prepare to return to the sea. Notice what Brendan is doing and how he speaks to each monk while the boat is loaded.

• Take a moment to look at the boat when it is fully loaded, paying attention to the shape and size of the boat as well as the equipment and how the supplies are stored for the journey. Then, see the young man come to them carrying a basket of bread, noting his appearance and actions as well as the responses of Brendan and his companions to him as he approaches them. Listen as Brendan and the young man bless each other, observing their actions and hearing their words. Notice the reactions of the monks to the conversation between their abbot and the young man.

• See and hear Brendan and his companions on the ocean — sometimes under sail and sometimes rowing when there is no wind — noting the shifts in their moods and their manner of speaking with one another. Look at Brendan during the journey, noticing the ways he guides and assures his fellow monks as they work on the boat. Observe any differences of attitude or demeanor among the monks as well as any shared behaviors in these different situations, noting how each looks to Brendan for leadership.

• See and hear the companions as they approach and land on

the Island of Sheep, noticing whether they land easily or with difficulty. Look around the island, noting its physical characteristics and the location of the sheep. Observe Brendan and the monks as they come ashore and take a lamb from the flock, noting how Brendan and his companions react when the steward of the island approaches them with a basket of bread as well as whether he joins them for their meal or leaves after giving them the bread.

• As you watch and listen to Brendan and his companions prepare their meal, focus your attention on Brendan. See what he does as the monks cook the lamb and prepare a place in which to eat, noting how he prepares for the meal. Take a moment to notice how he responds to the actions of his companions, observing those times when he participates with his companions and when he separates himself from them.

[3]   See the monks and the steward gather together when the meal is prepared and become aware that they are about to pray. Ask God to help you join in their prayer — allowing you to join with the monks or to listen quietly while they pray.

Then, slowly read Psalm 27: 1-14 while seeing and hearing Brendan and his companions chant the psalm in your imagination. You may find that particular phrases touch you more deeply than others. Or you may find specific images, memories and emotions — perhaps even sounds and fragrances — associated with the different parts of the psalm. Make a mental note of these things.

After the monks conclude their prayer, allow their image to fade from your imagination as you become aware of the particular phrases and images from the psalm which touched you most deeply. Recall the emotions and memories — as well as any sounds or smells — evoked by the words of the psalm. Allow these key aspects of your prayer to linger on your mind and in your heart, making a mental note of any special feelings evoked by them.

When you are ready, speak with God in an open and informal manner about how the psalm expresses your own needs or desires — giving space for God to respond or to highlight different aspects of the psalm. Gradually allow your thoughts to recede as you focus on God's presence in your life and in the world around you.

[4]   When you are ready, take a moment to gather any important thoughts, emotions and memories from this meditation before concluding with this prayer from Alexander Carmichael's *Carmina Gadelica*:

O God of life, darken not to me your light,
O God of life, close not to me your joy,
O God of life, shut not to me your door,
    O God of life, refuse not to me your mercy,
    O God of life, quench toward me your wrath,
    O God of life, crown me with your gladness,
O God of life, crown me with your gladness. Amen.

[5]   Take 5-10 minutes to reflect on the most significant moments from this time of prayer. Then, record your preliminary reflections in your journal.

Verses 1 through 11

[1]   Again, feel your desire to live in God's goodness so you may use the many gifts God has given you. Feeling God's continuing care to you, open yourself to the immense love God shows for you. Then, ask that you may be open to the divine presence all around you. Also, pray that you may trust in God's care and protection — giving you the courage to confront the many challenges you face in life.

As these desires fill your consciousness, allow all other concerns to fall aside as you focus on this specific time and place.

[2]   Then, when you are ready, slowly read the account of Jesus during the wedding feast at Cana in John 2: 1-11. As you read, you may find particular phrases from the passage touching you more deeply than others and want to concentrate on these for a while. Or you may find yourself focusing on images, memories and emotions — perhaps even sounds and fragrances — associated with the different parts of the reading.

Linger for a moment on any phrases or events in the reading that touched you deeply, noticing the feelings evoked by them.

[3]   Now, ask God to guide you into this moment in your imagination. Allow God to provide the words and actions that help place you in this moment with Jesus — whether becoming a part of the story or observing it. While you may refer to the biblical account during your prayer, do not be afraid if your imagination leads Jesus, his mother or other people at the wedding feast to expand their conversation during your prayer — adding different words or phrases, perhaps mirroring your own speech patterns.

• Watch Jesus and his disciples at the wedding feast, noting where they are seated and how they are dressed. Look at Jesus, observing the ways he interacts with his disciples and the other guests. Notice how the disciples and other guests treat Jesus and how Jesus engages the people around him.

• Take a moment to look at the location of the feast, paying attention to whether the celebration is in a large hall, under an outdoor awning or completely out-of-doors. See the wedding guests and how they are arranged, noting any differences among them — such as the quality of their clothing, the ways they interact with the other guests, or the attention they receive from the host. Look at the types of food and drink provided to the guests, observing how they are presented and the attitudes of the various guests as they consume them. Notice whether you feel heat or wind on your skin as well as whether you feel warm or cool.

• See and hear Mary at the feast, noting her appearance and actions as she discovers that there is no more wine. Listen as someone tells her about the wine and she speaks with Jesus, noticing Jesus' response to his mother and his demeanor throughout the conversation. Observe Mary and Jesus as they approach the servants, noting how they respond when Mary and Jesus speak with them.

• See and hear the servants as they follow Jesus' instructions, noticing whether they are eager or reluctant to obey Jesus. Listen to the servants as they fill the large jars and take them to the chief steward, hearing the response of the steward and his conversation with the bridegroom. Observe the reactions of the servants as they talk about the miracle they have just seen, noting whether they speak among themselves or share the story while serving the wine to the wedding guests.

Allow these images to fade from your imagination. Become aware of the emotions and memories that touched you most deeply — phrases or images, sounds or smells, etc. Make a mental note of any strong feelings evoked by these aspects of your prayer.

[4]   Then, see Jesus standing or sitting in front of you. Look at him — noting his physical characteristics and demeanor — as you become aware of your feelings as you are with him. Remember that Jesus wants to reveal himself to you, so try to be aware of his feelings as he is with you. Consider what you need to say to him about your recent prayer and open yourself to hear what he needs to say to you.

When you are ready, speak with Jesus as you would a close friend in an informal conversation. Allow your imagination to guide you freely as you speak, remaining open to changes in the topics of conversation and giving Jesus the space to introduce the issues and concerns from your recent prayer that he thinks are important for you to hear.

[5]   When you are ready, take a moment to gather any important thoughts, emotions and memories from this contemplation before concluding with this prayer:

O God of life, darken not to me your light,
O God of life, close not to me your joy,
O God of life, shut not to me your door,

O God of life, refuse not to me your mercy,
O God of life, quench toward me your wrath,
O God of life, crown me with your gladness,
O God of life, crown me with your gladness. Amen.

[6]   Again, take 5-10 minutes to reflect on the most significant moments from this time of prayer. Then, record your preliminary reflections in your journal.

A Repeated Contemplation of John 2

Verses 1 through 11

[1]   Again, feel your desire to live in God's goodness so you may use the many gifts God has given you. Feeling God's continuing care to you, open yourself to the immense love God shows for you. Then, ask that you may be open to the divine presence all around you. Also, pray that you may trust in God's care and protection — giving you the courage to confront the many challenges you face in life.

As these desires fill your consciousness, allow all other concerns to fall aside as you focus on this specific time and place.

[2]   Then, when you are ready, slowly re-read the account of Jesus during the wedding feast at Cana in John 2: 1-11. As you read, you again may find particular phrases from the passage touching you more deeply than others and want to concentrate on these for a while. Or you may find yourself focusing on images, memories and emotions — perhaps even sounds and fragrances — associated with the different parts of the reading.

Linger for a moment on any phrases or moments from the reading that touched you deeply, noticing the feelings evoked by them.

[3]   Now, ask God to guide you into this event in your imagination. Allow God to provide the words and actions that help place you in this moment with Jesus — whether becoming a part of the story or observing it. While you may refer to the biblical account during your prayer, do not be afraid if your imagination leads Jesus, his mother or other people at the wedding feast to expand their conversation during your prayer — adding different words or phrases, perhaps mirroring your own speech patterns.

Note: Allow your memories from your earlier contemplation of this episode to guide you back into Jesus' first miracle at Cana.

• Watch Jesus and his disciples at the wedding feast, noting where they are seated and how they are dressed. Look at Jesus, observing the ways he interacts with his disciples and the other guests. Notice how the disciples and other guests treat Jesus and how Jesus engages the people around him.

• Take a moment to look at the location of the feast, paying attention to whether the celebration is in a large hall, under an outdoor awning or completely out-of-doors. See the wedding guests and how they are arranged, noting any differences among them — such as the quality of their clothing, the ways they interact with the other guests, or the attention they receive from the host. Look at the types of food and drink provided to the guests, observing how they are presented and the attitudes of the various guests as they consume them. Notice whether you feel heat or wind on your skin as well as whether you feel warm or cool.

• See and hear Mary at the feast, noting her appearance and actions as she discovers that there is no more wine. Listen as someone tells her about the wine and she speaks with Jesus, noticing Jesus' response to his mother and his demeanor throughout the conversation. Observe Mary and Jesus as they approach the servants, noting how they respond when Mary and Jesus speak with them.

• See and hear the servants as they follow Jesus' instructions, noticing whether they are eager or reluctant to obey Jesus. Listen to the servants as they fill the large jars and take them to the chief steward, hearing the response of the steward and his conversation with the bridegroom. Observe the reactions of the servants as they talk about the miracle they have just seen, noting whether they speak among themselves or share the story while serving the wine to the wedding guests.

Allow these images to fade from your imagination. Become aware of the emotions and memories that touched you most deeply — phrases or images, sounds or smells, etc. Make a mental note of any strong feelings evoked by these aspects of your prayer.

[4]   Then, see Jesus standing or sitting in front of you. Look at him — noting his physical characteristics and demeanor — as you become aware of your feelings as you are with him. Remember that Jesus wants to reveal himself to you, so try to be aware of his feelings as he is with you. Consider what you need to say to him about your recent prayer and open yourself to hear what he needs to say to you.

When you are ready, speak with Jesus as you would a close friend in an informal conversation. Allow your imagination to guide you freely as you speak, remaining open to changes in the topics of conversation and giving Jesus the space to introduce the issues and concerns from your recent prayer that he thinks are important for you to hear.

[5]   When you are ready, take a moment to gather any important thoughts, emotions and memories from this contemplation before

concluding with this prayer:

O God of life, darken not to me your light,
O God of life, close not to me your joy,
O God of life, shut not to me your door,
> *O God of life, refuse not to me your mercy,*
> *O God of life, quench toward me your wrath,*
> *O God of life, crown me with your gladness,*
O God of life, crown me with your gladness. Amen.

[6]   Again, take 5-10 minutes to reflect on the most significant moments from this time of prayer. Then, record your preliminary reflections in your journal.

Verses 1 through 12

[1]   Again, feel your desire to live in God's goodness so you may use the many gifts God has given you. Feeling God's continuing care to you, open yourself to the immense love God shows for you. Then, ask that you may be open to the divine presence all around you. Also, pray that you may trust in God's care and protection — giving you the courage to confront the many challenges you face in life.

As these desires fill your consciousness, allow all other concerns to fall aside as you focus on this specific time and place.

[2]   Then, when you are ready, imagine Brendan and his companions leaving the Island of Sheep.

• Watch the steward of the island bring supplies to the monks, noting how he interacts with them as they prepare to leave the island. Watch the monks prepare the boat, observing the different attitudes of each monk as he prepares to set sail. Notice Brendan's demeanor as he guides his fellow monks in their work while speaking with the steward.

• Take a moment to watch Brendan and his companions as they leave the island, paying attention to their excitement as they continue their journey. Listen to the monks as they sail on the ocean, hearing the conversations between individual monks as well as any activities they conduct in common — such as singing or praying. Look at the sky and become aware of whether the day is sunny or cloudy, observing whether you feel warm or cool. Also, notice if you feel heat or wind on your skin.

• See and hear Brendan and his companions as they approach a barren island, noting the appearance of the shore and any objects you see on it. Watch as the boat comes to ground, noticing how the monks respond when they need to get out of the boat some distance from the shore. Observe Brendan as he remains in the boat, noting his actions while his companions pull the boat to land and take supplies ashore before going to sleep on the island.

• See and hear the monks as they wake and say their prayers in the morning, noticing what Brendan does as he remains in the boat. Watch as the island begins to shake and the monks struggle to get into the boat, seeing Brendan helping his companions. Observe the monks as they watch the island move away from them — with their fires still burning on it — and note their reactions as Brendan explains that the island on which they slept was actually a giant beast.

• As you watch Jasconius disappear into the distance, focus your attention on Brendan. See him reassure his companions and assuage their anxiety, noting how the monks respond to their abbot. Take a moment to notice Brendan's demeanor as he comforts his monks, observing the trust they show toward him in this moment.

[3]   Become aware that the monks are about to pray and ask God to help you join in their prayer — allowing you to join with the monks or to listen quietly while they pray.

Then, slowly read Psalm 62: 1-12 while seeing and hearing Brendan and his companions chant the psalm in your imagination. You may find that particular phrases touch you more deeply than others. Or you may find specific images, memories and emotions — perhaps even sounds and fragrances — associated with the different parts of the psalm. Make a mental note of these things.

After the monks conclude their prayer, allow their image to fade from your imagination as you become aware of the particular phrases and images from the psalm which touched you most deeply. Recall the emotions and memories — as well as any sounds or smells — evoked by the words of the psalm. Allow these key aspects of your prayer to linger on your mind and in your heart, making a mental note of any special feelings evoked by them.

When you are ready, speak with God in an open and informal manner about how the psalm expresses your own needs or desires — giving space for God to respond or to highlight different aspects of the psalm. Gradually allow your thoughts to recede as you focus on God's presence in your life and in the world around you.

[4]   When you are ready, take a moment to gather any important thoughts, emotions and memories from this meditation before concluding with this prayer:

> O God of life, darken not to me your light,
> O God of life, close not to me your joy,
> O God of life, shut not to me your door,
>> O God of life, refuse not to me your mercy,
>> O God of life, quench toward me your wrath,
>> O God of life, crown me with your gladness,
> O God of life, crown me with your gladness. Amen.

[5]   Again, take 5-10 minutes to reflect on the most significant moments from this time of prayer. Then, record your preliminary reflections in your journal.

An Application of the Senses

[1]   Again, feel your desire to live in God's goodness so you may use the many gifts God has given you. Feel God's continuing care as you open yourself to the immense love God shows for you and ask that you may be open to the divine presence all around you. Also, pray that you may trust in God's care and protection — giving you the courage to confront the many challenges you face in life.

Then, focus on this moment as all other concerns fade away.

[2]   When you are ready, using your imagination, bring to mind the experiences of Brendan and his companions on the Island of Sheep and during their encounter with Jasconius. Allow the images and words of these stories to linger and then slowly fade from your consciousness. Consider the images and feelings evoked in you during your prayer, feeling God's presence in these memories and becoming aware of the specific sensations associated with each image.

Then, in turn, remember your recent prayers on Psalm 27, Psalm 62 and Jesus at Cana. As these prayers enter your memory, make a mental note of which senses are most active. You may see an image or a color, hear a sound or a phrase, or smell a scent or a fragrance. You may even taste a flavor or feel a sensation on your skin.

Finally, relax and allow these various memories and experiences to quietly enter and leave your consciousness without being controlled — whether they are clear or diffuse, whether they come quickly or slowly. Linger on the sensory images and memories being evoked in you — noticing any images or colors, any sounds or phrases, any scents or fragrances, any flavors or physical sensations associated with each prayer.

[3]   When you are ready, become completely still and clear your mind of all thoughts and concerns. Watch as God forms a small image or object in your mind containing the most important gift you have been given during this particular time of prayer — the thought or awareness that you most need to carry with you into your life.

Reverently pick up the object or image, looking at it carefully and becoming aware of the divine presence contained within it. Take a moment to register what it looks like and how it feels in your hand. Then, feel the joy and confidence that comes from touching the presence of God as you accept this gift, offering a short prayer of gratitude while you relax into the pleasure of this moment.

[4]   Then, conclude by offering this prayer:

O God of life, darken not to me your light,
O God of life, close not to me your joy,
O God of life, shut not to me your door,
   O God of life, refuse not to me your mercy,
   O God of life, quench toward me your wrath,
   O God of life, crown me with your gladness,
O God of life, crown me with your gladness. Amen.

[5]   While your experiences are still fresh in your mind, record the most significant impressions or sensations from this time of prayer in your journal and thank God for the special gift you received from him.

[1]   Remember your desire to remain open to God's presence in everything around you so you might accept the many gifts that God gives you each day. Recall how you asked to trust in God's care and protection, giving you the courage to confront the many challenges you face in life. Then, take a moment to allow the words, thoughts and feelings from your prayers during the last day or week to linger — on your mind and in your heart — before asking God to reveal His presence in these various memories.

[2]   Think about the stories of Brendan and his companions on the Island of Sheep and during their encounter with Jasconius. Remember the parts of these stories that spoke most powerfully to you and think about how elements from them resurfaced in your recent prayers on Psalms 27 and 62 as well as on Jesus at Cana. Ask God to help you understand these moments.

[3]   Consider your meditations on Psalms 27 and 62. Recall the most powerful images, phrases or feelings from your prayers. Ask yourself what gifts God gave to you through these moments, perhaps offering you new insights or perhaps affirming an important aspect of your faith. Ask yourself how God may be calling you to change through these moments, being as specific as possible.

Examine your disposition as you prayed, noting whether prayer came easily or with resistance. Recall the easiest moments in your prayer and any moments of joy you may have experienced. Remember also if you encountered any difficulty opening yourself to God or if you felt any sadness as you prayed. Ask God to help you understand why these feelings surfaced.

Bring to mind any moments when you added personal elements — familiar places or people from your life — or connected your prayers to other scriptures or spiritual writings. Ask yourself how these additions helped or hindered you as you prayed. Again, if you do not know why this happened, ask God to help you understand.

[4]   Ponder your contemplation of Jesus at Cana, allowing a mental picture of this event to form in your mind as you recall the perspective from which you experienced it. Then, review your prayer in the same way as your earlier reflections on Psalms 27 and 62.

[5]   Recall the ebb and flow of sensory impressions and feelings that marked your application of the senses. Isolate the most memorable

moments and sensory impressions from your prayer and reflect on how God used these moments to give you a particular gift, perhaps offering you new insights or changing you in some way. Then, consider what you want to offer God in return for these moments.

[6]   Finally, remember the times when images or feelings from the readings of this day or week surfaced outside these prayer periods. Consider those moments or events in which God's presence or guidance was especially strong as well as any moments when you were struggling. Think about the most memorable aspects of these experiences, asking God to explain their significance.

[7]   Take a moment to allow the words, thoughts and feelings of these prayers to linger on your mind and in your heart. Then, conclude by asking for God's continued presence and guidance as you offer this prayer:

> *Bless to me, O God,*
>> *Each thing my eyes see;*
> *Bless to me, O God,*
>> *Each sound my ears hear;*
> *Bless to me, O God,*
>> *Each odor that goes to my nostrils;*
> *Bless to me, O God,*
>> *Each taste that goes to my lips;*
>> *Each note that goes to my song,*
>> *Each ray that guides my way,*
>> *Each thing that I pursue,*
>> *Each lure that tempts my will,*
>> *The zeal that seeks my living soul,*
> *The Three that seek my heart,*
>> *The zeal that seeks my living soul,*
> *The Three that seek my heart. Amen.*

[8]   After finishing these prayers, summarize your reflections on the gifts or graces you received during the prayers of this last day or week and record these insights in your journal. Then, being as specific as possible, you should conclude this summary with a short prayer of gratitude for God's generosity toward you during the previous day or week.

IV • THE PARADISE OF BIRDS

Preparation

Consideration of the Readings:
>	After attending or prayerfully reading the prayer service for this day or week:
>	• Read (or hear) "The Paradise of Birds" and its companion reflection, "Accepting Forgiveness as a Loved Sinner". Allow yourself to linger on any thoughts or phrases that seem particularly meaningful or relevant to your life. Then, record these moments in your workbook.
>	• Read Psalm 33. Again, pay careful attention to any phrases or images that seem particularly meaningful to you. Then, record these highlights from the psalm in your workbook so you will remember them during the meditations on these readings in this section of the retreat.
>	• Read about Jesus' encounter with the blind man in John 9: 1-41. Make a mental note of each person's appearance and actions during the episode as well as the key elements of the story, including the setting. Again, consider any aspects of this story that speak strongly to you and record these observations in your workbook.

>	*Note: You also should take a moment to consider any aspect of the prayer service from this day or week that seemed particularly significant to you.*

Contemplation of Your Needs:
>	When you are ready, concentrating on your breath or an object near you, allow any distractions to fade from your consciousness as you become aware of your desire to live in God's goodness. Feel yourself yearning to properly use the many gifts God has given you, to experience God's continuing care, and to be open to the immense love God shows for you.
>	Then, pray for your desires in the coming day or week. Ask God to deepen your companionship with Jesus, allowing you to feel the healing power of this relationship as it transforms your weaknesses into new and unexpected abilities. Also, pray that this may strengthen your faith by helping you love Jesus more dearly and follow Jesus more nearly — even in the most challenging situations. Allow these desires to linger on your mind and in your heart for a few moments before slowly reviewing your notes on the readings for the coming day or

week, asking God to be with you during these prayers — giving you the spiritual gifts you need from each of these readings as well as in your life after the retreat.

Finally, put your notes aside. Without straining your memory, consider in turn each of the readings for the coming day or week and allow them to take shape in your imagination — even if all you remember are small fragments. Prayerfully ponder how each reading affects you emotionally without overtly thinking about their content, asking God to illuminate the spiritual gifts offered in each reading — quieting your mind and creating a receptive space in yourself to see or hear the response.

Then, conclude by allowing these desires to fade from your consciousness as you offer this traditional prayer from Alexander Carmichael's *Carmina Gadelica*:

> *Bless to me, O God,*
> > *Each thing my eyes see;*
> *Bless to me, O God,*
> > *Each sound my ears hear;*
> *Bless to me, O God,*
> > *Each odor that goes to my nostrils;*
> *Bless to me, O God,*
> > *Each taste that goes to my lips;*
> > *Each note that goes to my song,*
> > *Each ray that guides my way,*
> > *Each thing that I pursue,*
> > *Each lure that tempts my will,*
> > *The zeal that seeks my living soul,*
> *The Three that seek my heart,*
> > *The zeal that seeks my living soul,*
> *The Three that seek my heart. Amen.*

Allow these words to linger on your mind and in your heart for a few moments and then, while they are still fresh in your memory, write the most important thoughts and feelings from this preparatory prayer in your workbook or journal.

Note: Remember to allow the dynamics of this preparation — the way it unfolded as well as any specific phrases or images that shaped it — to guide you into the later prayers in this section of your retreat.

Verses 1 through 9

[1]   Become aware of your desire to live in God's goodness so you may use the many gifts God has given you. Feel God's continuing care for you and open yourself to the immense love God shows for you. Then, ask God to deepen your companionship with Jesus and to strengthen your faith so you may love Jesus more dearly and follow Jesus more nearly — even in the most challenging situations.

As these desires fill your consciousness, allow all other concerns to fall aside as you focus on this specific time and place.

[2]   Then, when you are ready, join with Brendan and his companions in your imagination as they visit the Paradise of Birds.

• Watch Brendan and his companions sail along the coast of an island, noting whether the monks are straining as they work or being guided by a favorable wind. Look at the grass, trees and flowers on the island, observing the reactions of the monks to the beauty of the island. Notice the various ways Brendan speaks and acts as he guides the monks to the stream where they land their boat.

• Take a moment to watch and listen as Brendan instructs his companions to pull the boat — with him in it — against the current to the source of the stream, paying attention to whether the monks fulfill this task happily or grudgingly. Listen to the monks as they speak or sing while pulling the boat, noting how each monk responds to being on land once again. Look at Brendan sitting in the boat, observing his physical appearance as they approach a large tree at the source of the stream. Notice any differences between Brendan and his companions as they become aware that the tree is completely covered by white birds.

• See and hear Brendan as he asks God to explain the mystery of this huge tree and the birds on it, noting the intensity of his emotions as he prays. Listen to Brendan's prayer, hearing the words he uses and recognizing the relationship they reveal between God and Brendan. Observe the reaction of the other monks to Brendan's distress, noting whether the monks are confident or reticent as they try to comfort their abbot.

• See and hear one of the birds as it flies from the tree, noticing the beautiful bell-like sounds it makes. Watch Brendan's reaction as it alights on the prow of the boat, noticing the change in Brendan's behavior as he recognizes that the bird is a messenger from God. Listen to Brendan's conversation with the bird, noting the details of the birds' history — especially how it emphasizes their need for penance and God's generosity toward them.

• As the bird flies back to the tree, focus your attention on Brendan. Watch him as the bird leaves the boat as well as anything he says to his companions after the bird returns to the tree. Take a moment to notice Brendan's disposition as he reflects on his conversation with the bird, observing when his behavior differs from the other monks in his community.

[3]   As the sun sets, hear the birds beginning to chant and become of aware that Brendan and his companions plan to pray with them. Ask God to help you to share in this prayer, either joining them or listening quietly while they pray.

Then, slowly read Psalm 33: 1-9 while you imagine Brendan and his companions praying with the birds. You may find that particular phrases touch you more deeply than others. Or you may find specific images, memories and emotions — perhaps even sounds and fragrances — associated with the different parts of the psalm. Make a mental note of these things.

After the monks conclude their prayer, allow their image to fade from your imagination as you become aware of the particular phrases and images from the psalm which touched you most deeply. Recall the emotions and memories — as well as any sounds or smells — evoked by the words of the psalm. Allow these key aspects of your prayer to linger on your mind and in your heart, making a mental note of any special feelings evoked by them.

When you are ready, speak with God in an open and informal manner about how the psalm expresses your own needs or desires — giving space for God to respond or to highlight different aspects of the psalm. Gradually allow your thoughts to recede as you focus on God's presence in your life and in the world around you.

[4]   When you are ready, take a moment to gather any important thoughts, emotions and memories from this meditation before concluding with this prayer from Alexander Carmichael's *Carmina Gadelica*:

> *O God of life, darken not to me your light,*
> *O God of life, close not to me your joy,*
> *O God of life, shut not to me your door,*
>   *O God of life, refuse not to me your mercy,*

O God of life, quench toward me your wrath,
O God of life, crown me with your gladness,
O God of life, crown me with your gladness. Amen.

[5]   Take 5-10 minutes to reflect on this time of prayer. Then, record your preliminary reflections in your journal.

Verses 1 through 17

[1]   Again, feel your desire to live in God's goodness so you may use the many gifts God has given you. Feeling God's continuing care to you, open yourself to the immense love God shows for you. Then, ask God to deepen your companionship with Jesus and to strengthen your faith so you may love Jesus more dearly and follow Jesus more nearly — even in the most challenging situations.

As these desires fill your consciousness, allow all other concerns to fall aside as you focus on this specific time and place.

[2]   Then, when you are ready, slowly read the account of Jesus and the blind man in John 9: 1-17. As you read, you may find particular phrases from the passage touching you more deeply than others and want to concentrate on these for a while. Or you may find yourself focusing on images, memories and emotions — perhaps even sounds and fragrances — associated with the different parts of the reading.

Linger on any phrases or moments from the reading that touched you deeply, noticing the feelings evoked by them.

[3]   Now, ask God to guide you into this event in your imagination. Allow God to provide the words and actions that help place you in this moment with Jesus — whether becoming a part of the story or observing it. While you may refer to the biblical account during your prayer, do not be afraid if your imagination leads Jesus, the blind man or the other people in the episode to expand their conversation during your prayer — adding different words or phrases, perhaps mirroring your own speech patterns.

• Watch Jesus and his disciples walking down a road, noting the size of the group as well as the physical characteristics and activities of each member in the group. Look at the blind beggar sitting by the side of the road, observing his appearance and activities as Jesus and his disciples approach. Notice one of Jesus' disciples pointing at the beggar and speaking to Jesus.

• Take a moment to look at the road and the area around it, paying attention to the width and physical characteristics of the road as well as the vegetation near it or animals on it. See the people on the road — both with Jesus and anyone else passing by him on it — noting how close to the beggar people must come as they pass him. Look at the sky and become aware of whether the day is sunny or cloudy, observing whether the air feels humid or dry. Notice whether you feel heat or wind on your skin as well as whether you feel warm or cool.

   • See and hear Jesus and his disciples encounter the blind man and speak about him with Jesus, noting any differences in their attitudes and reactions to the man — within the group of disciples as well as between Jesus and his followers. Then, watch Jesus spit on the earth to make mud before spreading it on the man's eyes, listening to the words spoken by Jesus and the blind man and noticing the emotional effects of this conversation on both men. Observe the reactions to this conversation among Jesus' disciples and any other people on the road, noticing the emotional strength of these responses as well as whether they approve or disapprove of Jesus speaking with the beggar.

   • See and hear the beggar washing his eyes, noticing any changes in him as he regains his sight. Watch as different people question him and take him to the Pharisees, seeing the responses to the formerly blind man's story of Jesus restoring his sight. Observe the Pharisees as they question the man, noting confidence of the formerly blind man as he proclaims Jesus to be a prophet.

   Allow these images to fade from your imagination, becoming aware of the emotions and memories that touched you most deeply — phrases or images, sounds or smells, etc. Make a mental note of any strong feelings evoked by these aspects of your prayer.

[4]   Then, see Jesus standing or sitting in front of you. Look at him — noting his physical characteristics and demeanor — as you become aware of your feelings as you are with him. Remember that Jesus wants to reveal himself to you, so try to be aware of his feelings toward you. Consider what you need to say to him about your recent prayer and open yourself to hear what he needs to say to you.

   When you are ready, speak with Jesus as you would a close friend in an informal conversation. Allow your imagination to guide you freely as you speak, remaining open to changes in the topics of conversation and giving Jesus the space to introduce the issues and concerns from your recent prayer that he thinks are important for you to hear.

[5]   When you are ready, take a moment to gather any important thoughts, emotions and memories from this contemplation before concluding with this prayer:

   O God of life, darken not to me your light,
   O God of life, close not to me your joy,
   O God of life, shut not to me your door,

O God of life, refuse not to me your mercy,
O God of life, quench toward me your wrath,
O God of life, crown me with your gladness,
O God of life, crown me with your gladness. Amen.

[6]   Again, take 5-10 minutes to reflect on this time of prayer. Then, record your preliminary reflections in your journal.

Verses 1 through 41

[1]   Again, feel your desire to live in God's goodness so you may use the many gifts God has given you. Feeling God's continuing care to you, open yourself to the immense love God shows for you. Then, ask God to deepen your companionship with Jesus and to strengthen your faith so you may love Jesus more dearly and follow Jesus more nearly — even in the most challenging situations.

As these desires fill your consciousness, allow all other concerns to fall aside as you focus on this specific time and place.

[2]   Then, when you are ready, slowly read the account of Jesus and the blind man in John 9: 1-41. As you read, you may find particular phrases from the passage touching you more deeply than others and want to concentrate on these for a while. Or you may find yourself focusing on images, memories and emotions — perhaps even sounds and fragrances — associated with the different parts of the reading.

Linger on any phrases or moments from the reading that touched you deeply, noticing the feelings evoked by them.

[3]   Now, ask God to guide you into this event in your imagination. Allow God to provide the words and actions that help place you in this moment with Jesus — whether becoming a part of the story or observing it. While you may refer to the biblical account during your prayer, do not be afraid if your imagination leads Jesus, the blind man or other people in the episode to expand their conversation during your prayer — adding different words or phrases, perhaps mirroring your own speech patterns.

Note: *Allow your memories from your earlier contemplation of this episode to guide you back into Jesus' healing of the blind man.*

• Watch Jesus and his disciples walking down a road, noting the size of the group as well as the physical characteristics and activities of each member in the group. Look at the blind beggar sitting by the side of the road, observing his appearance and activities as Jesus and his disciples approach. Notice one of Jesus' disciples pointing at the beggar and speaking to Jesus.

• Take a moment to watch Jesus as he speaks with his disciples and the blind beggar, paying attention to his responses both to his own disciples and to the blind man. Then, watch Jesus spit on the earth to make mud before spreading it on the man's eyes, listening to the words spoken by Jesus and the blind man and noticing the emotional effects of this conversation on both men. Observe the reactions to this conversation among Jesus' disciples and any other people on the road, noting the emotional strength of these responses as well as whether they approve or disapprove of Jesus speaking with the beggar. Notice how Jesus responds to the various reactions as he watches the blind man leave.

> • See and hear the beggar washing his eyes, noting any changes in him as he regains his sight. Watch as different people question him and take him to the Pharisees, seeing the responses to the formerly blind man's story of Jesus restoring his sight. Observe the Pharisees as they question the man, noticing the confidence of the formerly blind man as he proclaims Jesus to be a prophet.

> • See and hear the Pharisees as they continue to question the man and his parents, noticing how they seek to undermine the man's testimony and the moral authority of Jesus. Listen to the Pharisees as they speak with the man and his parents, noticing the fear shown by his parents and the growing anger at the man as he remains firm in his testimony. Observe the man as he is expelled from his community, noting how Jesus seeks him out to reassure him and to challenge the actions of the Pharisees.

Allow these images to fade from your imagination, becoming aware of the emotions and memories that touched you most deeply — phrases or images, sounds or smells, etc. Make a mental note of any strong feelings evoked by these aspects of your prayer.

[4]   Then, see Jesus standing or sitting in front of you. Look at him — noting his physical characteristics and demeanor — as you become aware of your feelings as you are with him. Remember that Jesus wants to reveal himself to you, so try to be aware of his feelings toward you. Consider what you need to say to him about your recent prayer and open yourself to hear what he needs to say to you.

When you are ready, speak with Jesus as you would a close friend in an informal conversation. Allow your imagination to guide you freely as you speak, remaining open to changes in the topics of conversation and giving Jesus the space to introduce the issues and concerns from your recent prayer that he thinks are important for you to hear.

[5]   When you are ready, take a moment to gather any important

thoughts, emotions and memories from this contemplation before concluding with this prayer:

O God of life, darken not to me your light,
O God of life, close not to me your joy,
O God of life, shut not to me your door,
>*O God of life, refuse not to me your mercy,*
>*O God of life, quench toward me your wrath,*
>*O God of life, crown me with your gladness,*
O God of life, crown me with your gladness. Amen.

[6]   Again, take 5-10 minutes to reflect on this time of prayer. Then, record your preliminary reflections in your journal.

A repeated meditation on Psalm 33

Verses 1 through 22

[1]   Again, feel your desire to live in God's goodness so you may use the many gifts God has given you. Feeling God's continuing care to you, open yourself to the immense love God shows for you. Then, ask God to deepen your companionship with Jesus and to strengthen your faith so you may love Jesus more dearly and follow Jesus more nearly — even in the most challenging situations.

As these desires fill your consciousness, allow all other concerns to fall aside as you focus on this specific time and place.

[2]   Then, when you are ready, bring to mind your previous prayer on the monks' visit to the Paradise of Birds and allow it to shape your meditation on Psalm 33.

• Watch Brendan and his companions sail along the coast of an island, noting whether the monks are straining as they work or being guided by a favorable wind. Look at the grass, trees and flowers on the island, observing the reactions of the monks to the beauty of the island. Notice the various ways Brendan speaks and acts as he guides the monks to the stream where they land their boat.

• Take a moment to watch and listen as Brendan instructs his companions to pull the boat — with him in it — against the current to the source of the stream, paying attention to whether the monks fulfill this task happily or grudgingly. Listen to the monks as they speak or sing while pulling the boat, noting how each monk responds to being on land once again. Look at Brendan sitting in the boat, observing his physical appearance as they approach a large tree at the source of the stream. Notice any differences between Brendan and his companions as they become aware that the tree is completely covered by white birds.

• See and hear Brendan as he asks God to explain the mystery of this huge tree and the birds on it, noting the intensity of his emotions as he prays. Listen to Brendan's prayer, hearing the words he uses and recognizing the relationship they reveal between God and Brendan. Observe the reaction of the other monks to Brendan's distress, noting whether the monks are confident or reticent as they try to comfort their abbot.

• See and hear one of the birds as it flies from the tree, noticing the beautiful bell-like sounds it makes. Watch Brendan's reaction as it alights on the prow of the boat, noticing the change in Brendan's behavior as he recognizes that the bird is a messenger from God. Listen to Brendan's conversation with the bird, noting the details of the birds' history — especially how it emphasizes their need for penance and God's generosity toward them.

• As the bird flies back to the tree, focus your attention on Brendan. Watch him as the bird leaves the boat as well as anything he says to his companions after the bird returns to the tree. Take a moment to notice Brendan's disposition as he reflects on his conversation with the bird, observing when his behavior differs from the other monks in his community.

[3] As the sun sets, hear the birds beginning to chant and become of aware that Brendan and his companions plan to pray with them. Ask God to help you to share in this prayer, either joining them or listening quietly while they pray.

Then, slowly read Psalm 33: 1-22 while you imagine Brendan and his companions praying with the birds. You may find that particular phrases touch you more deeply than others. Or you may find specific images, memories and emotions — perhaps even sounds and fragrances — associated with the different parts of the psalm. Make a mental note of these things.

After the monks conclude their prayer, allow their image to fade from your imagination as you become aware of the particular phrases and images from the psalm which touched you most deeply. Recall the emotions and memories — as well as any sounds or smells — evoked by the words of the psalm. Allow these key aspects of your prayer to linger on your mind and in your heart, making a mental note of any special feelings evoked by them.

When you are ready, speak with God in an open and informal manner about how the psalm expresses your own needs or desires — giving space for God to respond or to highlight different aspects of the psalm. Gradually allow your thoughts to recede as you focus on God's presence in your life and in the world around you.

[4] When you are ready, take a moment to gather any important thoughts, emotions and memories from this meditation before concluding with this prayer:

O God of life, darken not to me your light,
O God of life, close not to me your joy,
O God of life, shut not to me your door,
    O God of life, refuse not to me your mercy,

O God of life, quench toward me your wrath,
O God of life, crown me with your gladness,
O God of life, crown me with your gladness. Amen.

[5]   Again, take 5-10 minutes to reflect on this time of prayer. Then, record your preliminary reflections in your journal.

An Application of the Senses

[1]   Again, feel your desire to live in God's goodness so you may use the many gifts God has given you. Feel God's continuing care as you open yourself to the immense love God shows for you. Then, ask God to deepen your companionship with Jesus and to strengthen your faith so you may love Jesus more dearly and follow Jesus more nearly — even in the most challenging situations.

Then, focus on this moment as all other concerns fade away.

[2]   When you are ready, using your imagination, consider Brendan's visit to the Paradise of Birds. Allow the images and words of this story to linger and then slowly fade from your consciousness. Consider the images and feelings evoked in you during your prayer, feeling God's presence in these memories and becoming aware of the specific sensations associated with each image.

Then, in turn, remember your recent prayers on Psalm 33 and Jesus with the blind man. As these prayers enter your memory, make a mental note of which senses are most active. You may see an image or a color, hear a sound or a phrase, or smell a scent or a fragrance. You may even taste a flavor or feel a sensation on your skin.

Finally, relax and allow these various memories and experiences to quietly enter and leave your consciousness without being controlled — whether they are clear or diffuse, whether they come quickly or slowly. Linger on the sensory images and memories being evoked in you — noticing any images or colors, any sounds or phrases, any scents or fragrances, any flavors or physical sensations associated with each prayer.

[3]   When you are ready, become completely still and clear your mind of all thoughts and concerns. Watch as God forms a small image or object in your mind containing the most important gift you have been given during this particular time of prayer — the thought or awareness that you most need to carry with you into your life.

Reverently pick up the object or image, looking at it carefully and becoming aware of the divine presence contained within it. Take a moment to register what it looks like and how it feels in your hand. Then, feel the joy and confidence that comes from touching the presence of God as you accept this gift, offering a short prayer of gratitude while you relax into the pleasure of this moment.

[4]   Then, conclude by offering this prayer:

O God of life, darken not to me your light,
O God of life, close not to me your joy,
O God of life, shut not to me your door,
    O God of life, refuse not to me your mercy,
    O God of life, quench toward me your wrath,
    O God of life, crown me with your gladness,
O God of life, crown me with your gladness. Amen.

[5]   While your experiences are still fresh in your mind, record the most significant impressions or sensations from this time of prayer in your journal and thank God for the special gift you received from him.

Review

[1]   Remember your desire to deepen your companionship with Jesus, transforming your weaknesses into new and unexpected abilities. Recall how you asked for the faith to love Jesus more dearly and follow Jesus more nearly, even in the most challenging situations. Then, take a moment to allow the words, thoughts and feelings from your prayers during the last day or week to linger — on your mind and in your heart — before asking God to reveal His presence in these various memories.

[2]   Think about Brendan's visit to the Paradise of Birds. Remember the parts of the story that spoke most powerfully to you and think about how elements of this story resurfaced in your recent prayers on Psalm 139 and Jesus' encounter with the blind man. Ask God to help you understand these moments.

[3]   Consider your meditations on Psalm 33. Recall the most powerful images, phrases or feelings from your prayer. Ask yourself what gifts God gave to you through these moments, perhaps offering you new insights or perhaps affirming an important aspect of your faith. Ask yourself how God may be calling you to change through these moments, being as specific as possible.

Examine your disposition as you prayed, noting whether prayer came easily or with resistance. Recall the easiest moments in your prayer and any moments of joy you may have experienced. Remember also if you encountered any difficulty opening yourself to God or if you felt any sadness as you prayed. Ask God to help you understand why these feelings surfaced.

Bring to mind any moments when you added personal elements — familiar places or people from your life — or connected your prayers to other scriptures or spiritual writings. Ask yourself how these additions helped or hindered you as you prayed. Again, if you do not know why this happened, ask God to help you understand.

[4]   Ponder your contemplation of Jesus with the blind man, allowing a mental picture of these events to form in your mind as you recall the perspective from which you experienced them. Then, review your prayer in the same way as your earlier reflection on Psalm 33.

[5]   Recall the ebb and flow of sensory impressions and feelings that marked your application of the senses. Isolate the most memorable moments and sensory impressions from your prayer and reflect on how God used these moments to give you a particular gift, perhaps offering

you new insights or changing you in some way. Then, consider what you want to offer God in return for these moments.

[6]   Finally, remember the times when images or feelings from the readings of this day or week surfaced outside these prayer periods. Consider those moments or events in which God's presence or guidance was especially strong as well as any moments when you were struggling. Think about the most memorable aspects of these experiences, asking God to explain their significance.

[7]   Take a moment to allow the words, thoughts and feelings of these prayers to linger on your mind and in your heart. Then, conclude by asking for God's continued presence and guidance as you offer this prayer:

> Bless to me, O God,
>> Each thing my eyes see;
> Bless to me, O God,
>> Each sound my ears hear;
> Bless to me, O God,
>> Each odor that goes to my nostrils;
> Bless to me, O God,
>> Each taste that goes to my lips;
>> Each note that goes to my song,
>> Each ray that guides my way,
>> Each thing that I pursue,
>> Each lure that tempts my will,
>> The zeal that seeks my living soul,
> The Three that seek my heart,
>> The zeal that seeks my living soul,
> The Three that seek my heart. Amen.

[8]   After finishing these prayers, summarize the most significant moments, insights or desires from this last day or week in your journal before concluding these reflections in a short prayer of gratitude for the specific gifts or graces received during your prayers.

V • THE COMMUNITY OF AILBE

Preparation

Consideration of the Readings:

After attending or prayerfully reading the prayer service for this day or week:

• Read (or hear) "The Community of Ailbe" and its companion reflection, "Living as Citizens of Heaven". Allow yourself to linger on any thoughts or phrases that seem particularly meaningful or relevant to your life. Then, record these moments in your workbook.

• Read Psalm 103. Again, pay careful attention to any phrases or images that seem particularly meaningful to you. Then, record these highlights from the psalm in your workbook so you will remember them during the meditations on these readings in this section of the retreat.

• Read about the miracle of the loaves and fishes (and the events that followed) in John 6: 1-21. Make a mental note of each person's appearance and actions during the episode as well as the key elements of the story, including the setting. Again, consider any aspects of this story that speak strongly to you and record these observations in your workbook.

Note: *You also should take a moment to consider any aspect of the prayer service from this day or week that seemed particularly significant to you.*

Contemplation of Your Needs:

When you are ready, concentrating on your breath or an object near you, allow any distractions to fade from your consciousness as you become aware of your desire to live in God's goodness. Feel yourself yearning to properly use the many gifts God has given you, to experience God's continuing care, and to be open to the immense love God shows for you.

Then, pray for your desires in the coming day or week. Ask God to deepen your companionship with Jesus, increasing your awareness of the various ways this relationship sustains your ability to love and follow Jesus when you feel weakened by fear or despair. Also, pray that this may nourish your deepest emotional and spiritual needs as you strive to live as a witness to God's love. Allow these desires to linger on your mind and in your heart for a few moments before slowly reviewing your notes on the readings for the coming day or week, asking God to be with you during these prayers — giving you the spiritual gifts you need from each of these readings as well as in your life after the retreat.

Finally, put your notes aside. Without straining your memory, consider in turn each of the readings for the coming day or week and allow them to take shape in your imagination — even if all you remember are small fragments. Prayerfully ponder how each reading affects you emotionally without overtly thinking about their content, asking God to illuminate the spiritual gifts offered in each reading — quieting your mind and creating a receptive space in yourself to see or hear the response.

Then, conclude by allowing these desires to fade from your consciousness as you offer this traditional prayer from Alexander Carmichael's *Carmina Gadelica*:

> Bless to me, O God,
>> Each thing my eyes see;
> Bless to me, O God,
>> Each sound my ears hear;
> Bless to me, O God,
>> Each odor that goes to my nostrils;
> Bless to me, O God,
>> Each taste that goes to my lips;
>> Each note that goes to my song,
>> Each ray that guides my way,
>> Each thing that I pursue,
>> Each lure that tempts my will,
>> The zeal that seeks my living soul,
> The Three that seek my heart,
>> The zeal that seeks my living soul,
> The Three that seek my heart. Amen.

Allow these words to linger on your mind and in your heart for a few moments and then, while they are still fresh in your memory, write the most important thoughts and feelings from this preparatory prayer in your workbook or journal.

Note: Remember to allow the dynamics of this preparation to guide you into the later prayers in this section of your retreat.

A Contemplation of John 6

Verses 1 through 21

[1]   Become aware of your desire to live in God's goodness so you may use the many gifts God has given you. Feel God's continuing care for you and open yourself to the immense love God shows for you. Then, ask God to deepen your companionship with Jesus — praying that this may nourish your deepest emotional and spiritual needs as you strive to live as a witness to God's love.

As these desires fill your consciousness, allow all other concerns to fall aside as you focus on this specific time and place.

[2]   Then, when you are ready, slowly about the miracle of the loaves and fishes (and the events that followed) in John 6: 1-21. As you read, you may find particular phrases from the passage touching you more deeply than others and want to concentrate on these for a while. Or you may find yourself focusing on images, memories and emotions — perhaps even sounds and fragrances — associated with the different parts of the reading.

Linger on any phrases or moments from the reading that touched you deeply, noticing the feelings evoked by them.

[3]   Now, ask God to guide you into this event in your imagination. Allow God to provide the words and actions that help place you in this moment with Jesus — whether becoming a part of the story or observing it. While you may refer to the biblical account during your prayer, do not be afraid if your imagination leads Jesus, the disciples or people in the crowd to expand their conversation during your prayer — adding different words or phrases, perhaps mirroring your own speech patterns.

• Watch Jesus sitting with his disciples on a hill near the shore of the Sea of Galilee, noting each person's physical characteristics and mannerisms as well as any emotions expressed by Jesus or his disciples as they spend this time together. Look at the people gathering around Jesus, observing how some try to get close to him and others remain at a distance. Notice the various ways people arrive as well as any changes in mood — among Jesus and his disciples or among the people approaching Jesus — as the crowd becomes larger.

• Take a moment to look at the hillside, paying attention to its physical characteristics and its distance from the Sea of Galilee. See the various groups gathered on the hill and along the shore, noting the differences in vegetation and terrain as well as any distinctive qualities among the people. Look at the sky and become aware of whether the day is sunny or cloudy, becoming aware of whether the air feels humid or dry. Notice whether you feel heat or wind on your skin as well as whether you feel warm or cool.

• See and hear Jesus speaking with his disciples about buying food for the crowd, noting the different responses of Philip and Andrew. Listen to Jesus as he tells his disciples to gather the people in small groups while taking the bread and fish he has been offered, noticing the different reactions among his disciples and among the people around Jesus. Observe Jesus' actions as he feeds the crowd and note his growing concern to the response of the crowd — and his disciples — to this miracle.

• See and hear Jesus as he withdraws from his disciples and the crowd to pray, noticing how he leaves and if anyone notices where he goes. Listen to the disciples as evening comes and they decide to leave without Jesus, hearing the different concerns voiced within the group and watching the various ways Jesus' disciples interact with the people gathered near them. See the disciples in their boat as the storm builds, noting their growing fear and how this changes when they see Jesus walking on the water toward them.

As Jesus enters the boat and the storm calms, allow these images to fade from your imagination. Become aware of the emotions and memories that touched you most deeply — phrases or images, sounds or smells, etc. Make a mental note of any strong feelings evoked by these aspects of your prayer.

[4]   Then, see Jesus standing or sitting in front of you. Look at him — noting his physical characteristics and demeanor — as you become aware of your feelings as you are with him. Remember that Jesus wants to reveal himself to you, so try to be aware of his feelings toward you. Consider what you need to say to him about your recent prayer and open yourself to hear what he needs to say to you.

When you are ready, speak with Jesus as you would a close friend in an informal conversation. Allow your imagination to guide you freely as you speak, remaining open to changes in the topics of conversation and giving Jesus the space to introduce the issues and concerns from your recent prayer that he thinks are important for you to hear.

[5]   When you are ready, take a moment to gather any important thoughts, emotions and memories from this contemplation before

concluding with this prayer from Alexander Carmichael's *Carmina Gadelica*:

> *O God of life, darken not to me your light,*
> *O God of life, close not to me your joy,*
> *O God of life, shut not to me your door,*
>> *O God of life, refuse not to me your mercy,*
>> *O God of life, quench toward me your wrath,*
>> *O God of life, crown me with your gladness,*
> *O God of life, crown me with your gladness. Amen.*

[6]   Take 5-10 minutes to reflect on this time of prayer. Then, record your preliminary reflections in your journal.

A Repeated Contemplation of John 6

Verses 1 through 40

[1]   Again, feel your desire to live in God's goodness so you may use the many gifts God has given you. Feeling God's continuing care to you, open yourself to the immense love God shows for you. Then, ask God to deepen your companionship with Jesus — praying that this may nourish your deepest emotional and spiritual needs as you strive to live as a witness to God's love.

As these desires fill your consciousness, allow all other concerns to fall aside as you focus on this specific time and place.

[2]   Then, when you are ready, slowly read about the miracle of the loaves and fishes (and the events that followed) in John 6: 1-40. As you read, you may find particular phrases from the passage touching you more deeply than others and want to concentrate on these for a while. Or you may find yourself focusing on images, memories and emotions — perhaps even sounds and fragrances — associated with the different parts of the reading.

Linger on any phrases or moments from the reading that touched you deeply, noticing the feelings evoked by them.

[3]   Now, ask God to guide you into this event in your imagination. Allow God to provide the words and actions that help place you in this moment with Jesus — whether becoming a part of the story or observing it. While you may refer to the biblical account during your prayer, do not be afraid if your imagination leads Jesus, the disciples or people in the crowd to expand their conversation during your prayer — adding different words or phrases, perhaps mirroring your own speech patterns.

Note: Allow your memories from your earlier contemplation of this episode to help place you with Jesus during your prayer.

• Watch Jesus sitting with his disciples on a hill near the shore of the Sea of Galilee, noting each person's physical characteristics and mannerisms as well as any emotions expressed by Jesus or his disciples as they spend this time together. Look at the people gathering around Jesus, observing how some try to get close to him and others remain at a distance. Notice the various ways people arrive as well as any changes in mood as the crowd becomes larger.

• Take a moment to listen as Jesus speaks with his disciples about buying food for the crowd, paying attention to the different responses of Philip and Andrew. Hear Jesus tell his disciples to gather the people in small groups while taking the bread and fish he has been offered, noting the different reactions among his disciples and among the people around Jesus. See Jesus as he feeds the crowd — observing the various ways that Jesus' disciples and the people gathered around them respond to this miracle. Notice how Jesus becomes concerned by their response to his actions and withdraws from the crowd to pray.

• See and hear the disciples as they decide to leave without Jesus, noting the different concerns voiced within the group and watching the various ways the disciples interact with the people gathered near them. Watch the disciples get into their boat and leave without Jesus, noticing their growing fear as the storm builds and threatens to capsize their boat. Observe Jesus as he walks on the water toward the disciples and gets into the boat, noting the various reactions among the disciples as they storm diminishes and the water calms around them.

• See and hear the people as they return to Capernaum, noticing their surprise when they discover Jesus. Listen to some people as they question how Jesus managed to return from the other side of the Sea of Galilee when they saw his disciples leave without him, hearing the various explanations offered by different members of the crowd. Observe some people as they approach Jesus and ask why he had left them, noting Jesus' emotional response to their questions before hearing him address the crowd.

When Jesus finishes speaking, allow these images to fade from your imagination. Become aware of the emotions and memories that touched you most deeply — phrases or images, sounds or smells, etc. Make a mental note of any strong feelings evoked by these aspects of your prayer.

[4]   Then, see Jesus standing or sitting in front of you. Look at him — noting his physical characteristics and demeanor — as you become aware of your feelings as you are with him. Remember that Jesus wants to reveal himself to you, so try to be aware of his feelings toward you. Consider what you need to say to him about your recent prayer and open yourself to hear what he needs to say to you.

When you are ready, speak with Jesus as you would a close friend in an informal conversation. Allow your imagination to guide you freely as you speak, remaining open to changes in the topics of conversation and giving Jesus the space to introduce the issues and concerns from your recent prayer that he thinks are important for you to hear.

[5]   When you are ready, take a moment to gather any important thoughts, emotions and memories from this contemplation before concluding with this prayer:

O God of life, darken not to me your light,

O God of life, close not to me your joy,

O God of life, shut not to me your door,

    O God of life, refuse not to me your mercy,

    O God of life, quench toward me your wrath,

    O God of life, crown me with your gladness,

O God of life, crown me with your gladness. Amen.

[6]   Again, take 5-10 minutes to reflect on this time of prayer. Then, record your preliminary reflections in your journal.

Verses 1 through 14

[1]   Again, feel your desire to live in God's goodness so you may use the many gifts God has given you. Feeling God's continuing care to you, open yourself to the immense love God shows for you. Then, ask God to deepen your companionship with Jesus — praying that this may nourish your deepest emotional and spiritual needs as you strive to live as a witness to God's love.

As these desires fill your consciousness, allow all other concerns to fall aside as you focus on this specific time and place.

[2]   Then, when you are ready, imagine Brendan and his companions as they visit the Community of Ailbe.

• Watch Brendan and his companions struggle to land on an island, noting how exhausted they appear as they scramble onto land. See the monks rush toward two wells near the shore, observing Brendan's reaction to their behavior and hearing him forbid them to take any water from the wells. Notice the different responses of the monks as they listen to their abbot.

• Take a moment look at the terrain of the island, paying attention to whether it is lush with vegetation or desolate and stony. Look at the two wells, noting the clear water in one and the muddy water in the other as well as their construction and any pathways leading to or from them. Look at the sky and become aware of whether the day is sunny or cloudy, becoming aware of whether the air feels humid or dry. Notice whether you feel heat or wind on your skin as well as whether you feel warm or cool.

• See an old but sturdy monk approach the group and prostrate himself before Brendan, noting Brendan's attempts to question the monk after raising him to his feet. Listen to Brendan telling his companions not to speak while they are on this island, watching as the monk guides the travelers to his monastery. Observe the other monks greeting Brendan and his companions and sharing a meal with the visitors in silence, noticing the physical characteristics of the dining room and how the monks — both hosts and guests — are arranged as well as how they interact with one another.

• See and hear the abbot of the island welcome — and chastise — the visitors, noticing his physical appearance and mannerisms as well as Brendan's reactions to the abbot as he speaks. Watch the entire group leave the dining room and process into the chapel, looking carefully at the arrangement and decoration of the room. Observe the behavior of both the host and guest monks as they take their places and wait for the two abbots to take their places in the chapel, noting how Brendan's companions sometimes seem familiar with the practices of their hosts and sometimes seem confused by them.

• As the abbot of the island sits near the center of the chapel, focus your attention on Brendan and where he is sitting. Watch him as he looks around the chapel, noting his responses to the physical characteristics of the chapel and the prayerfulness of the joined communities of monks. Take a moment to notice how he responds to the actions around him, observing any changes in his emotional disposition or demeanor.

[3]   Aware that the monks are about to pray, ask God to help you join in their prayer — allowing you to join with the monks or to listen quietly while they pray.

Then, slowly read Psalm 103: 1-14 while seeing and hearing the two communities chant the psalm together in your imagination. You may find that particular phrases touch you more deeply than others. Or you may find specific images, memories and emotions — perhaps even sounds and fragrances — associated with the different parts of the psalm. Make a mental note of these things.

After the monks conclude their prayer, allow their image to fade from your imagination as you become aware of the particular phrases and images from the psalm which touched you most deeply. Recall the emotions and memories — as well as any sounds or smells — evoked by the words of the psalm. Allow these key aspects of your prayer to linger on your mind and in your heart, making a mental note of any special feelings evoked by them.

When you are ready, speak with God in an open and informal manner about how the psalm expresses your own needs or desires — giving space for God to respond or to highlight different aspects of the psalm. Gradually allow your thoughts to recede as you focus on God's presence in your life and in the world around you.

[4]   When you are ready, take a moment to gather any important thoughts, emotions and memories from this meditation before concluding with this prayer:

O God of life, darken not to me your light,
O God of life, close not to me your joy,
O God of life, shut not to me your door,

O God of life, refuse not to me your mercy,
O God of life, quench toward me your wrath,
O God of life, crown me with your gladness,
O God of life, crown me with your gladness. Amen.

[5]   Again, take 5-10 minutes to reflect on this time of prayer. Then, record your preliminary reflections in your journal.

A repeated meditation on Psalm 103

Verses 1 through 22

[1]   Again, feel your desire to live in God's goodness so you may use the many gifts God has given you. Feeling God's continuing care to you, open yourself to the immense love God shows for you. Then, ask God to deepen your companionship with Jesus — praying that this may nourish your deepest emotional and spiritual needs as you strive to live as a witness to God's love.

As these desires fill your consciousness, allow all other concerns to fall aside as you focus on this specific time and place.

[2]   Then, when you are ready, imagine Brendan and his companions as they visit the Community of Ailbe.

• Watch Brendan and his companions struggle to land on an island, noting how exhausted they appear as they scramble onto land. See the monks rush toward two wells near the shore, observing Brendan's reaction to their behavior and hearing him forbid them to take any water from the wells. Notice the different responses of the monks as they listen to their abbot.

• Take a moment look at the terrain of the island, paying attention to whether it is lush with vegetation or desolate and stony. Look at the two wells, noting the clear water in one and the muddy water in the other as well as their construction and any pathways leading to or from them. Look at the sky and become aware of whether the day is sunny or cloudy, becoming aware of whether the air feels humid or dry. Notice whether you feel heat or wind on your skin as well as whether you feel warm or cool.

• See an old but sturdy monk approach the group and prostrate himself before Brendan, noting Brendan's attempts to question the monk after raising him to his feet. Listen to Brendan telling his companions not to speak while they are on this island, watching as the monk guides the travelers to his monastery. Observe the other monks greeting Brendan and his companions and sharing a meal with the visitors in silence, noticing the physical characteristics of the dining room and how the monks — both hosts and guests — are arranged as well as how they interact with one another.

• See and hear the abbot of the island welcome — and chastise — the visitors, noticing his physical appearance and mannerisms as well as Brendan's reactions to the abbot as he speaks. Watch the entire group leave the dining room and process into the chapel, looking carefully at the arrangement and decoration of the room. Observe the behavior of both the host and guest monks as they take their places and wait for the two abbots to take their places in the chapel, noting how Brendan's companions sometimes seem familiar with the practices of their hosts and sometimes seem confused by them.

• As the abbot of the island sits near the center of the chapel, focus your attention on Brendan and where he is sitting. Watch him as he looks around the chapel, noting his responses to the physical characteristics of the chapel and the prayerfulness of the joined communities of monks. Take a moment to notice how he responds to the actions around him, observing any changes in his emotional disposition or demeanor.

[3]   Aware that the monks are about to pray, a ask God to help you join in their prayer — allowing you to join with the monks or to listen quietly while they pray.

Then, slowly read Psalm 103: 1-22 while you imagine the two communities chanting the psalm together. You may find that particular phrases touch you more deeply than others. Or you may find specific images, memories and emotions — perhaps even sounds and fragrances — associated with the different parts of the psalm. Make a mental note of these things.

After the monks conclude their prayer, allow their image to fade from your imagination as you become aware of the particular phrases and images from the psalm which touched you most deeply. Recall the emotions and memories — as well as any sounds or smells — evoked by the words of the psalm. Allow these key aspects of your prayer to linger on your mind and in your heart, making a mental note of any special feelings evoked by them.

When you are ready, speak with God in an open and informal manner about how the psalm expresses your own needs or desires — giving space for God to respond or to highlight different aspects of the psalm. Gradually allow your thoughts to recede as you focus on God's presence in your life and in the world around you.

[4]   When you are ready, take a moment to gather any important thoughts, emotions and memories from this meditation before concluding with this prayer:

> O God of life, darken not to me your light,
> O God of life, close not to me your joy,
> O God of life, shut not to me your door,

O God of life, refuse not to me your mercy,
O God of life, quench toward me your wrath,
O God of life, crown me with your gladness,
O God of life, crown me with your gladness. Amen.

[5]   Again, take 5-10 minutes to reflect on this time of prayer. Then, record your preliminary reflections in your journal.

An Application of the Senses

[1]   Again, feel your desire to live in God's goodness so you may use the many gifts God has given you. Feel God's continuing care as you open yourself to the immense love God shows for you and ask God to deepen your companionship with Jesus — praying that this may nourish your deepest emotional and spiritual needs as you strive to live as a witness to God's love.

[2]   When you are ready, using your imagination, recall Brendan's visit to the Community of Ailbe. Allow the images and words of this story to linger and then slowly fade from your consciousness. Consider the images and feelings evoked in you during your prayer, feeling God's presence in these memories and becoming aware of the specific sensations associated with each image.

Then, in turn, remember your recent prayers on Psalm 103 and the miracles of the loaves and fishes (and the events that followed it). As these prayers enter your memory, make a mental note of which senses are most active. You may see an image or a color, hear a sound or a phrase, or smell a scent or a fragrance. You may even taste a flavor or feel a sensation on your skin.

Finally, relax and allow these various memories and experiences to quietly enter and leave your consciousness without being controlled — whether they are clear or diffuse, whether they come quickly or slowly. Linger on the sensory images and memories being evoked in you — noticing any images or colors, any sounds or phrases, any scents or fragrances, any flavors or physical sensations associated with each prayer.

[3]   When you are ready, become completely still and clear your mind of all thoughts and concerns. Watch as God forms a small image or object in your mind containing the most important gift you have been given during this particular time of prayer — the thought or awareness that you most need to carry with you into your life.

Reverently pick up the object or image, looking at it carefully and becoming aware of the divine presence contained within it. Take a moment to register what it looks like and how it feels in your hand. Then, feel the joy and confidence that comes from touching the presence of God as you accept this gift, offering a short prayer of gratitude while you relax into the pleasure of this moment.

[4]   Then, conclude by offering this prayer:

O God of life, darken not to me your light,
O God of life, close not to me your joy,
O God of life, shut not to me your door,
    O God of life, refuse not to me your mercy,
    O God of life, quench toward me your wrath,
    O God of life, crown me with your gladness,
O God of life, crown me with your gladness. Amen.

[5]   While your experiences are still fresh in your mind, record the most significant impressions or sensations from this time of prayer in your journal and thank God for the special gift you received from him.

Review

[1]   Remember your desire to deepen your companionship with Jesus, increasing your awareness of how this relationship sustains your ability to love and follow Jesus when you feel weakened by fear or despair. Recall how you asked for this to nourish your deepest emotional and spiritual needs as you strive to live as a witness to God's love. Then, take a moment to allow the words, thoughts and feelings from your prayers during the last day or week to linger — on your mind and in your heart — before asking God to reveal His presence in these various memories.

[2]   Think about Brendan and his companions as they visited the Community of Ailbe. Remember the parts of the story that spoke most powerfully to you and think about how elements of this story resurfaced in your recent prayers on Psalm 103 and the miracle of the loaves and fishes (as well as the events around it). Ask God to help you understand these moments.

[3]   Consider your meditations on Psalm 103. Recall the most powerful images, phrases or feelings from your prayer. Ask yourself what gifts God gave to you through these moments, perhaps offering you new insights or perhaps affirming an important aspect of your faith. Ask yourself how God may be calling you to change through these moments, being as specific as possible.

Examine your disposition as you prayed, noting whether prayer came easily or with resistance. Recall the easiest moments in your prayer and any moments of joy you may have experienced. Remember also if you encountered any difficulty opening yourself to God or if you felt any sadness as you prayed. Ask God to help you understand why these feelings surfaced.

Bring to mind any moments when you added personal elements — familiar places or people from your life — or connected your prayers to other scriptures or spiritual writings. Ask yourself how these additions helped or hindered you as you prayed. Again, if you do not know why this happened, ask God to help you understand.

[4]   Ponder your contemplation of miracles of the loaves and fishes (and the events that followed it), allowing a mental picture of these events to form in your mind as you recall the perspective from which you experienced them. Then, review your prayer in the same way as your earlier reflection on Psalm 103.

[5]   Recall the ebb and flow of sensory impressions and feelings that marked your application of the senses. Isolate the most memorable moments and sensory impressions from your prayer and reflect on how God used these moments to give you a particular gift, perhaps offering you new insights or changing you in some way. Then, consider what you want to offer God in return for these moments.

[6]   Finally, remember the times when images or feelings from the readings of this day or week surfaced outside these prayer periods. Consider those moments or events in which God's presence or guidance was especially strong as well as any moments when you were struggling. Think about the most memorable aspects of these experiences, asking God to explain their significance.

[7]   Take a moment to allow the words, thoughts and feelings of these prayers to linger on your mind and in your heart. Then, conclude by asking for God's continued presence and guidance as you offer this prayer:

> Bless to me, O God,
>> Each thing my eyes see;
> Bless to me, O God,
>> Each sound my ears hear;
> Bless to me, O God,
>> Each odor that goes to my nostrils;
> Bless to me, O God,
>> Each taste that goes to my lips;
>> Each note that goes to my song,
>> Each ray that guides my way,
>> Each thing that I pursue,
>> Each lure that tempts my will,
>> The zeal that seeks my living soul,
> The Three that seek my heart,
>> The zeal that seeks my living soul,
> The Three that seek my heart. Amen.

[8]   After finishing these prayers, summarize the most significant moments, insights or desires from this last day or week in your journal before concluding these reflections in a short prayer of gratitude for the specific gifts or graces received during your prayers.

VI • THE CRYSTAL PILLAR
& THE ISLAND OF SMITHS

Preparation

Consideration of the Readings:

After attending or prayerfully reading the prayer service for this day or week:

• Read (or hear) "The Crystal Pillar & The Island of Smiths" and its companion reflection, "Learning the Patterns of God's Presence". Allow yourself to linger on any thoughts or phrases that seem particularly meaningful or relevant to your life. Then, record these moments in your workbook.

• Read Psalm 40. Again, pay careful attention to any phrases or images that seem particularly meaningful to you. Then, record these highlights from the psalm in your workbook so you will remember them during the meditations on these readings in this section of the retreat.

• Read about Jesus raising Lazarus from the dead in John 11: 1-3, 17-46. Make a mental note of each person's appearance and actions during the episode as well as the key elements of the story, including the setting. Again, consider any aspects of this story that speak strongly to you and record these observations in your workbook.

Note: You also should take a moment to consider any aspect of the prayer service from this day or week that seemed particularly significant to you.

Contemplation of Your Needs:

When you are ready, concentrating on your breath or an object near you, allow any distractions to fade from your consciousness as you become aware of your desire to live in God's goodness. Feel yourself yearning to properly use the many gifts God has given you, to experience God's continuing care, and to be open to the immense love God shows for you.

Then, pray for your desires in the coming day or week. Ask God to deepen your companionship with Jesus, praying for the humility to accept the healing power of this relationship when you stumble back into old sinful habits. Also, pray to recognize the many gifts Jesus offers each day to renew your efforts to live as a sign of hope in the world. Allow these desires to linger on your mind and in your heart for a few moments before slowly reviewing your notes on the readings for the coming day or week, asking God to be with you during these prayers — giving you the spiritual gifts you need from each of these readings as well as in your life after the retreat.

Finally, put your notes aside. Without straining your memory, consider in turn each of the readings for the coming day or week and allow them to take shape in your imagination — even if all you remember are small fragments. Prayerfully ponder how each reading affects you emotionally without overtly thinking about their content, asking God to illuminate the spiritual gifts offered in each reading — quieting your mind and creating a receptive space in yourself to see or hear the response.

Then, conclude by allowing these desires to fade from your consciousness as you offer this traditional prayer from Alexander Carmichael's *Carmina Gadelica*:

> *Bless to me, O God,*
> > *Each thing my eyes see;*
> *Bless to me, O God,*
> > *Each sound my ears hear;*
> *Bless to me, O God,*
> > *Each odor that goes to my nostrils;*
> *Bless to me, O God,*
> > *Each taste that goes to my lips;*
> > *Each note that goes to my song,*
> > *Each ray that guides my way,*
> > *Each thing that I pursue,*
> > *Each lure that tempts my will,*
> > *The zeal that seeks my living soul,*
> > *The Three that seek my heart,*
> > *The zeal that seeks my living soul,*
> > *The Three that seek my heart. Amen.*

Allow these words to linger on your mind and in your heart for a few moments and then, while they are still fresh in your memory, write the most important thoughts and feelings from this preparatory prayer in your workbook or journal.

Note: Remember to allow the dynamics of this preparation to guide you into the later prayers in this section of your retreat.

Verses 1 through 12

[1]   Become aware of your desire to live in God's goodness so you may use the many gifts God has given you. Feel God's continuing care for you and open yourself to the immense love God shows for you. Then, ask God to deepen your companionship with Jesus so you may live as a sign of hope in the world. Also, pray for the humility to accept God's forgiveness when you stumble back into sinful habits.

As these desires fill your consciousness, allow all other concerns to fall aside as you focus on this specific time and place.

[2]   Then, when you are ready, imagine encountering the Crystal Tower and the Island of Smiths with Brendan and his companions:

• Watch Brendan and his companions approach a large object emerging from the ocean, seeing the monks express their surprise that it took three days to reach the tower — which they thought was nearby when they first saw it. Look at Brendan and his companions as they approach the Crystal Tower, observing the different reactions among the monks as they near the netting that covers the tower. Notice whether the monks feel relieved or tense as they come closer to the tower and how they turn to their abbot for guidance and reassurance.

• Take a moment to look at the tower, paying attention to how it extends deep into the clear ocean as well as far into the sky and is covered with a silver-like netting. See how light illuminates the tower and reflects off the netting, noting any patterns in the shape of the tower or the construction of its covering. Become aware of whether the day is sunny or cloudy as you look up toward the top of the tower before looking down into the ocean, observing any sea birds in the air and any fish in the water. Notice whether you feel heat or wind on your skin as well as whether you feel warm or cool.

• See and hear Brendan tell his companions to sail through the netting and to approach the tower, noting the different reactions of the monks — especially Brendan — toward the object. Look at Brendan and his companions as they explore the tower and carefully measure each of its four sides, noticing Brendan's sense of wonder when they find a chalice and paten made from the same material as the netting over the tower. Observe Brendan and his companions as they navigate their boat out of the netting, noticing how they catch a favorable wind that guides them away from the tower.

• See and hear Brendan as he tells the other monks that they must avoid the barren island they are approaching, noticing its rough and rocky terrain covered with fiery forges and piles of slag. Hear the thunder-like sound of bellows coming from the island, noting the reactions of the monks when an angry inhabitant of the island picks up and heats a piece of slag in his forge before throwing it at their boat. Smell the putrid smoke of the island and hear howling from the island as its inhabitants come to the shore and kindle their own forges, watching the monks struggle to change their course while pieces of hot slag splash in the water around them.

• As the water around the boat seems to boil, focus your attention on Brendan. See him prayerfully guiding and reassuring his companions in the midst of this struggle, noting his composure amidst the chaos and his trust that God will guide them to safety. Take a moment to notice the tone of Brendan's voice as the waters around the boat become calm and he tells his fellow monks that they were in Hell.

[3]   Then, hear Brendan instruct his companion monks to pray and ask God to help you join in their prayer — allowing you to join with the monks or to listen quietly while they pray.

Then, slowly read Psalm 40: 1-12 while seeing and hearing Brendan and his companions chant the psalm in your imagination. You may find that particular phrases touch you more deeply than others. Or you may find specific images, memories and emotions — perhaps even sounds and fragrances — associated with the different parts of the psalm. Make a mental note of these things.

After the monks conclude their prayer, allow their image to fade from your imagination as you become aware of the particular phrases and images from the psalm which touched you most deeply. Recall the emotions and memories — as well as any sounds or smells — evoked by the words of the psalm. Allow these key aspects of your prayer to linger on your mind and in your heart, making a mental note of any special feelings evoked by them.

When you are ready, speak with God in an open and informal manner about how the psalm expresses your own needs or desires — giving space for God to respond or to highlight different aspects of the psalm. Gradually allow your thoughts to recede as you focus on God's presence in your life and in the world around you.

[4]   When you are ready, take a moment to gather any important thoughts, emotions and memories from this meditation before concluding with this prayer from Alexander Carmichael's *Carmina*

Gadelica:

> *O God of life, darken not to me your light,*
> *O God of life, close not to me your joy,*
> *O God of life, shut not to me your door,*
>> *O God of life, refuse not to me your mercy,*
>> *O God of life, quench toward me your wrath,*
>> *O God of life, crown me with your gladness,*
> *O God of life, crown me with your gladness. Amen.*

[5]   Take 5-10 minutes to reflect on this time of prayer. Then, record your preliminary reflections in your journal.

A Contemplation of John 11

Verses 1 through 3, continuing with verses 17 through 46

[1]   Again, feel your desire to live in God's goodness so you may use the many gifts God has given you. Feeling God's continuing care to you, open yourself to the immense love God shows for you. Then, ask God to deepen your companionship with Jesus so you may live as a sign of hope in the world. Also, pray for the humility to accept God's forgiveness when you stumble back into sinful habits.

As these desires fill your consciousness, allow all other concerns to fall aside as you focus on this specific time and place.

[2]   Then, when you are ready, slowly read the account of Jesus raising Lazarus from the dead in John 11: 1-3, 17-46. As you read, you may find particular phrases from the passage touching you more deeply than others and want to concentrate on these for a while. Or you may find yourself focusing on images, memories and emotions — perhaps even sounds and fragrances — associated with the different parts of the reading.

Linger on any phrases or moments from the reading that touched you deeply, noticing the feelings evoked by them.

[3]   Now, ask God to guide you into this event in your imagination. Allow God to provide the words and actions that help place you in this moment with Jesus — whether becoming a part of the story or observing it. While you may refer to the biblical account during your prayer, do not be afraid if your imagination leads Jesus, Martha, Mary or other people in the crowd to expand their conversation during your prayer — adding different words or phrases, perhaps mirroring your own speech patterns.

• Take a moment to see Jesus arriving at Bethany, paying attention to the buildings in the town and the people who have come to console Lazarus' two sisters. See the reaction of the crowd to Jesus and watch as a person comes up to tell him of Lazarus' death, noting Jesus' reaction to this news and the various responses of people in the crowd gathered around him. Look at the sky and become aware of whether the day is sunny or cloudy, observing whether the air feels humid or dry. Notice whether you feel heat or wind on your skin as well as whether you feel warm or cool as you approach Lazarus' home.

• See and hear Martha come out of the house to greet Jesus, noting her appearance and mannerisms as she talks to him about her brother and listens to Jesus as he speaks about the resurrection. See Martha go back into the house so that Mary may also greet Jesus, noticing whether Mary comes out alone or ahead of Martha as well as any differences in appearance or behavior between the sisters. Observe Mary as she kneels at Jesus' feet before speaking to him and see how Jesus responds to her, noting the reactions of the sisters and the crowd when Jesus asks to be taken to the tomb.

 • See and hear Jesus, the two sisters and other mourners approach the tomb and listen as Jesus asks that the stone be removed from its entrance, noticing the reactions of the two sisters, Jesus' disciples and the rest of the crowd as Jesus prays and calls Lazarus from the tomb. See Lazarus come out of the tomb, watching the excitement and reluctance of Mary and Martha — and the other people around Jesus — as he instructs them to remove Lazarus' burial wrappings be removed. Look at Lazarus as the wrappings are removed from his body, observing the actions of Jesus and noting the different responses from Lazarus' sisters, Jesus' disciples and the crowd to this miracle.

As these images fade from your imagination, become aware of the emotions and memories that touched you most deeply — phrases or images, sounds or smells, etc. Make a mental note of any strong feelings evoked by these aspects of your prayer.

[4]   Then, see Jesus standing or sitting in front of you. Look at him — noting his physical characteristics and demeanor — as you become aware of your feelings as you are with him. Remember that Jesus wants to reveal himself to you, so try to be aware of his feelings toward you. Consider what you need to say to him about your recent prayer and open yourself to hear what he needs to say to you.

When you are ready, speak with Jesus as you would a close friend in an informal conversation. Allow your imagination to guide you freely as you speak, remaining open to changes in the topics of conversation and giving Jesus the space to introduce the issues and concerns from your recent prayer that he thinks are important for you to hear.

[5]   When you are ready, take a moment to gather any important thoughts, emotions and memories from this contemplation before concluding with this prayer:

> O God of life, darken not to me your light,
> O God of life, close not to me your joy,
> O God of life, shut not to me your door,
>   O God of life, refuse not to me your mercy,

114

O God of life, quench toward me your wrath,
O God of life, crown me with your gladness,
O God of life, crown me with your gladness. Amen.

[6]   Again, take 5-10 minutes to reflect on this time of prayer. Then, record your preliminary reflections in your journal.

Verses 1 through 17

[1]   Again, feel your desire to live in God's goodness so you may use the many gifts God has given you. Feeling God's continuing care to you, open yourself to the immense love God shows for you. Then, ask God to deepen your companionship with Jesus so you may live as a sign of hope in the world. Also, pray for the humility to accept God's forgiveness when you stumble back into sinful habits.

As these desires fill your consciousness, allow all other concerns to fall aside as you focus on this specific time and place.

[2]   Then, when you are ready, imagine encountering the Crystal Tower and the Island of Smiths with Brendan and his companions:

• Watch Brendan and his companions approach a large object emerging from the ocean, seeing the monks express their surprise that it took three days to reach the tower — which they thought was nearby when they first saw it. Look at Brendan and his companions as they approach the Crystal Tower, observing the different reactions among the monks as they near the netting that covers the tower. Notice whether the monks feel relieved or tense as they come closer to the tower and how they turn to their abbot for guidance and reassurance.

• Take a moment to look at the tower, paying attention to how it extends deep into the clear ocean as well as far into the sky and is covered with a silver-like netting. See how light illuminates the tower and reflects off the netting, noting any patterns in the shape of the tower or the construction of its covering. Become aware of whether the day is sunny or cloudy as you look up toward the top of the tower before looking down into the ocean, observing any sea birds in the air and any fish in the water. Notice whether you feel heat or wind on your skin as well as whether you feel warm or cool.

• See and hear Brendan tell his companions to sail through the netting and to approach the tower, noting the different reactions of the monks — especially Brendan — toward the object. Look at Brendan and his companions as they explore the tower and carefully measure each of its four sides, noticing Brendan's sense of wonder when they find a chalice and paten made from the same material as the netting. Observe Brendan and his companions as they navigate their boat away from the tower, noticing their reactions when they catch a favorable wind.

• See and hear Brendan as he tells the other monks that they must avoid the barren island they are approaching, noticing its rough and rocky terrain covered with fiery forges and piles of slag. Hear the thunder-like sound of bellows coming from the island, noting the reactions of the monks when an angry inhabitant of the island picks up and heats a piece of slag in his forge before throwing it at their boat. Smell the putrid smoke of the island and hear howling from the island as its inhabitants come to the shore and kindle their own forges, watching the monks struggle to change their course while pieces of hot slag splash in the water around them.

• As the water around the boat seems to boil, focus your attention on Brendan. See him prayerfully guiding and reassuring his companions in the midst of this struggle, noting his composure amidst the chaos and his trust that God will guide them to safety. Take a moment to notice the tone of Brendan's voice as the waters around the boat become calm and he tells his fellow monks that they were in Hell.

[3]　　Then, hear Brendan instruct his companion monks to pray and ask God to help you join in their prayer — allowing you to join with the monks or to listen quietly while they pray.

Then, slowly read Psalm 40: 1-17 while you imagine Brendan and his companions chanting the psalm. You may find that particular phrases touch you more deeply than others. Or you may find specific images, memories and emotions — perhaps even sounds and fragrances — associated with the different parts of the psalm. Make a mental note of these things.

After the monks conclude their prayer, allow their image to fade from your imagination as you become aware of the particular phrases and images from the psalm which touched you most deeply. Recall the emotions and memories — as well as any sounds or smells — evoked by the words of the psalm. Allow these key aspects of your prayer to linger on your mind and in your heart, making a mental note of any special feelings evoked by them.

When you are ready, speak with God in an open and informal manner about how the psalm expresses your own needs or desires — giving space for God to respond or to highlight different aspects of the psalm. Gradually allow your thoughts to recede as you focus on God's presence in your life and in the world around you.

[4]　　When you are ready, take a moment to gather any important thoughts, emotions and memories from this meditation before concluding with this prayer:

O God of life, darken not to me your light,
O God of life, close not to me your joy,
O God of life, shut not to me your door,
  O God of life, refuse not to me your mercy,
  O God of life, quench toward me your wrath,
  O God of life, crown me with your gladness,
O God of life, crown me with your gladness. Amen.

[5] Again, take 5-10 minutes to reflect on this time of prayer. Then, record your preliminary reflections in your journal.

A Repeated Contemplation of John 11

Verses 1 through 3, continuing with verses 17 through 46

[1]   Again, feel your desire to live in God's goodness so you may use the many gifts God has given you. Feeling God's continuing care to you, open yourself to the immense love God shows for you. Then, ask God to deepen your companionship with Jesus so you may live as a sign of hope in the world. Also, pray for the humility to accept God's forgiveness when you stumble back into sinful habits.

As these desires fill your consciousness, allow all other concerns to fall aside as you focus on this specific time and place.

[2]   Then, when you are ready, slowly read the account of Jesus raising Lazarus from the dead in John 11: 1-3, 17-46. As you read, you may find particular phrases from the passage touching you more deeply than others and want to concentrate on these for a while. Or you may find yourself focusing on images, memories and emotions — perhaps even sounds and fragrances — associated with the different parts of the reading.

Linger on any phrases or moments from the reading that touched you deeply, noticing the feelings evoked by them.

[3]   Now, ask God to guide you into this event in your imagination. Allow God to provide the words and actions that help place you in this moment with Jesus — whether becoming a part of the story or observing it. While you may refer to the biblical account during your prayer, do not be afraid if your imagination leads Jesus, Martha, Mary or other people in the crowd to expand their conversation during your prayer — adding different words or phrases, perhaps mirroring your own speech patterns.

Note: *Allow your memories from your earlier contemplation of this episode to help place you with Jesus as he raises Lazarus from the dead.*

• Take a moment to see Jesus arriving at Bethany, paying attention to the buildings in the town and the people who have come to console Lazarus' two sisters. See the reaction of the crowd to Jesus and watch as a person comes up to tell him of Lazarus' death, noting Jesus' reaction to this news and the various responses of people in the crowd gathered around him. Look at the sky and become aware of whether the day is sunny or cloudy, observing whether the air feels humid or dry. Notice whether you feel heat or wind on your skin as well as whether you feel warm or cool as you approach Lazarus' home.

• See and hear Martha come out of the house to greet Jesus, noting her appearance and mannerisms as she talks to him about her brother and listens to Jesus as he speaks about the resurrection. See Martha go back into the house so that Mary may also greet Jesus, noticing whether Mary comes out alone or ahead of Martha as well as any differences in appearance or behavior between the sisters. Observe Mary as she kneels at Jesus' feet before speaking to him and see how Jesus responds to her, noting the reactions of the sisters and the crowd when Jesus asks to be taken to the tomb.

• See and hear Jesus, the two sisters and other mourners approach the tomb and listen as Jesus asks that the stone be removed from its entrance, noticing the reactions of the two sisters, Jesus' disciples and the rest of the crowd as Jesus prays and calls Lazarus from the tomb. See Lazarus come out of the tomb, watching the excitement and reluctance of Mary and Martha — and the other people around Jesus — as he instructs them to remove Lazarus' burial wrappings be removed. Look at Lazarus as the wrappings are removed from his body, observing the actions of Jesus and noting the different responses from Lazarus' sisters, Jesus' disciples and the crowd to this miracle.

As these images fade from your imagination, become aware of the emotions and memories that touched you most deeply — phrases or images, sounds or smells, etc. Make a mental note of any strong feelings evoked by these aspects of your prayer.

[4]   Then, see Jesus standing or sitting in front of you. Look at him — noting his physical characteristics and demeanor — as you become aware of your feelings as you are with him. Remember that Jesus wants to reveal himself to you, so try to be aware of his feelings toward you. Consider what you need to say to him about your recent prayer and open yourself to hear what he needs to say to you.

When you are ready, speak with Jesus as you would a close friend in an informal conversation. Allow your imagination to guide you freely as you speak, remaining open to changes in the topics of conversation and giving Jesus the space to introduce the issues and concerns from your recent prayer that he thinks are important for you to hear.

[5]   When you are ready, take a moment to gather any important thoughts, emotions and memories from this contemplation before

concluding with this prayer:

> *O God of life, darken not to me your light,*
> *O God of life, close not to me your joy,*
> *O God of life, shut not to me your door,*
>> *O God of life, refuse not to me your mercy,*
>> *O God of life, quench toward me your wrath,*
>> *O God of life, crown me with your gladness,*
> *O God of life, crown me with your gladness. Amen.*

[6]   Again, take 5-10 minutes to reflect on this time of prayer. Then, record your preliminary reflections in your journal.

An Application of the Senses

[1]   Again, feel your desire to live in God's goodness so you may use the many gifts God has given you. Feel God's continuing care as you open yourself to the immense love God shows for you and ask God to deepen your companionship with Jesus so you may live as a sign of hope in the world. Also, pray for the humility to accept God's forgiveness when you stumble back into sinful habits.

Then, focus on this moment as all other concerns fade away.

[2]   When you are ready, using your imagination, bring to mind the stories of Brendan and his companions at the Crystal Tower and near the Island of Smiths. Allow the images and words of these stories to linger and then slowly fade from your consciousness. Consider the images and feelings evoked in you during your prayer, feeling God's presence in these memories and becoming aware of the specific sensations associated with each image.

Then, in turn, remember your recent prayers on Psalm 40 and Jesus raising Lazarus from the dead. As these prayers enter your memory, make a mental note of which senses are most active. You may see an image or a color, hear a sound or a phrase, or smell a scent or a fragrance. You may even taste a flavor or feel a sensation on your skin.

Finally, relax and allow these various memories and experiences to quietly enter and leave your consciousness without being controlled — whether they are clear or diffuse, whether they come quickly or slowly. Linger on the sensory images and memories being evoked in you — noticing any images or colors, any sounds or phrases, any scents or fragrances, any flavors or physical sensations associated with each prayer.

[3]   When you are ready, become completely still and clear your mind of all thoughts and concerns. Watch as God forms a small image or object in your mind containing the most important gift you have been given during this particular time of prayer — the thought or awareness that you most need to carry with you into your life.

Reverently pick up the object or image, looking at it carefully and becoming aware of the divine presence contained within it. Take a moment to register what it looks like and how it feels in your hand. Then, feel the joy and confidence that comes from touching the presence of God as you accept this gift, offering a short prayer of gratitude while you relax into the pleasure of this moment.

[4]   Then, conclude by offering this prayer:
        O God of life, darken not to me your light,
        O God of life, close not to me your joy,
        O God of life, shut not to me your door,
                O God of life, refuse not to me your mercy,
                O God of life, quench toward me your wrath,
                O God of life, crown me with your gladness,
        O God of life, crown me with your gladness. Amen.
[5]   While your experiences are still fresh in your mind, record the
most significant impressions or sensations from this time of prayer in
your journal and thank God for the special gift you received from him.

Review

[1]   Remember your desire that God arouse in you deeper remorse and sorrow for your sins. Recall how you asked that you might share in Jesus' grief and brokenness during his Passion — as well as his deep sense of compassion, even for those that harmed him. Then, take a moment to allow the words, thoughts and feelings from your prayers during the last day or week to linger — on your mind and in your heart — before asking God to reveal His presence in these various memories.

[2]   Think about the stories of Brendan and his companions at the Crystal Tower and near the Island of Smiths. Remember the parts of these stories that spoke most powerfully to you and think about how elements from them resurfaced in your recent prayers on Psalm 40 and Jesus raising Lazarus from the dead. Ask God to help you understand these moments.

[3]   Consider your meditations on Psalm 40. Recall the most powerful images, phrases or feelings from your prayer. Ask yourself what gifts God gave to you through these moments, perhaps offering you new insights or perhaps affirming an important aspect of your faith. Ask yourself how God may be calling you to change through these moments, being as specific as possible.

Examine your disposition as you prayed, noting whether prayer came easily or with resistance. Recall the easiest moments in your prayer and any moments of joy you may have experienced. Remember also if you encountered any difficulty opening yourself to God or if you felt any sadness as you prayed. Ask God to help you understand why these feelings surfaced.

Bring to mind any moments when you added personal elements — familiar places or people from your life — or connected your prayers to other scriptures or spiritual writings. Ask yourself how these additions helped or hindered you as you prayed. Again, if you do not know why this happened, ask God to help you understand.

[4]   Ponder your contemplation of Jesus raising Lazarus from the dead, allowing a mental picture of this event to form in your mind as you recall the perspective from which you experienced it. Then, review your prayer in the same way as your earlier reflection on Psalm 40.

[5]   Recall the ebb and flow of sensory impressions and feelings that marked your application of the senses. Isolate the most memorable moments and sensory impressions from your prayer and reflect on how

God used these moments to give you a particular gift, perhaps offering you new insights or changing you in some way. Then, consider what you want to offer God in return for these moments.

[6]   Finally, remember the times when images or feelings from the readings of this day or week surfaced outside these prayer periods. Consider those moments or events in which God's presence or guidance was especially strong as well as any moments when you were struggling. Think about the most memorable aspects of these experiences, asking God to explain their significance.

[7]   Take a moment to allow the words, thoughts and feelings of these prayers to linger on your mind and in your heart. Then, conclude by asking for God's continued presence and guidance as you offer this prayer:

> Bless to me, O God,
> > Each thing my eyes see;
> Bless to me, O God,
> > Each sound my ears hear;
> Bless to me, O God,
> > Each odor that goes to my nostrils;
> Bless to me, O God,
> > Each taste that goes to my lips;
> > Each note that goes to my song,
> > Each ray that guides my way,
> > Each thing that I pursue,
> > Each lure that tempts my will,
> > The zeal that seeks my living soul,
> > The Three that seek my heart,
> > The zeal that seeks my living soul,
> > The Three that seek my heart. Amen.

[8]   After finishing these prayers, summarize the most significant moments, insights or desires from this last day or week in your journal before concluding these reflections in a short prayer of gratitude for the specific gifts or graces received during your prayers.

VII • UNHAPPY JUDAS

Preparation

Consideration of the Readings:

After attending or prayerfully reading the prayer service for this day or week:

• Read (or hear) "Unhappy Judas" and its companion reflection, "Embracing the Standard of Christ". Allow yourself to linger on any thoughts or phrases that seem particularly meaningful or relevant to your life. Then, record these moments in your workbook.

• Read Psalm 22. Again, pay careful attention to any phrases or images that seem particularly meaningful to you. Then, record these highlights from the psalm in your workbook so you will remember them during the meditations on these readings in this section of the retreat.

• Read the selected passages on the Passion of Jesus from John 18: 1 through John 19: 30. Make a mental note of each person's appearance and actions during the episode as well as the key elements of the story, including the setting. Again, record in your workbook any aspects of this story that speak strongly to you.

Note: You also should take a moment to consider any aspect of the prayer service from this day or week that seemed particularly significant to you.

Contemplation of Your Needs:

When you are ready, concentrating on your breath or an object near you, allow any distractions to fade from your consciousness as you become aware of your desire to live in God's goodness. Feel yourself yearning to properly use the many gifts God has given you, to experience God's continuing care, and to be open to the immense love God shows for you.

Then, pray for your desires in the coming day or week. Ask God to arouse in you deeper remorse and sorrow for your sins. Also, pray that you might share in Jesus' grief and brokenness during his Passion — as well as his deep sense of compassion, even for those that harmed him. Allow these desires to linger on your mind and in your heart for a few moments before slowly reviewing your notes on the readings for the coming day or week, asking God to be with you during these prayers — giving you the spiritual gifts you need from each of these readings as well as in your life after the retreat.

Finally, put your notes aside. Without straining your memory, consider in turn each of the readings for the coming day or week and allow them to take shape in your imagination — even if all you remember are small fragments. Prayerfully ponder how each reading affects you emotionally without overtly thinking about their content, asking God to illuminate the spiritual gifts offered in each reading — quieting your mind and creating a receptive space in yourself to see or hear the response.

Then, conclude by allowing these desires to fade from your consciousness as you offer this traditional prayer from Alexander Carmichael's *Carmina Gadelica*:

> Bless to me, O God,
> > Each thing my eyes see;
> Bless to me, O God,
> > Each sound my ears hear;
> Bless to me, O God,
> > Each odor that goes to my nostrils;
> Bless to me, O God,
> > Each taste that goes to my lips;
> > Each note that goes to my song,
> > Each ray that guides my way,
> > Each thing that I pursue,
> > Each lure that tempts my will,
> > The zeal that seeks my living soul,
> > The Three that seek my heart,
> > The zeal that seeks my living soul,
> > The Three that seek my heart. Amen.

Allow these words to linger on your mind and in your heart for a few moments and then, while they are still fresh in your memory, write the most important thoughts and feelings from this preparatory prayer in your workbook or journal.

Note: Remember to allow the dynamics of this preparation to guide you into the later prayers in this section of your retreat.

Verses 1 through 14, continuing with verses 19 through 24

[1]   Become aware of your desire to live in God's goodness so you may use the many gifts God has given you. Feel God's continuing care for you and open yourself to the immense love God shows for you. Then, ask God to arouse in you deeper remorse and sorrow for your sins. Also, pray that you might share in Jesus' grief and brokenness during his Passion — as well as his deep sense of compassion, even for those that harmed him.

As these desires fill your consciousness, allow all other concerns to fall aside as you focus on this specific time and place.

[2]   Then, when you are ready, slowly read the account of Jesus' arrest in John 18: 1-14, 19-24. As you read, you may find particular phrases from the passage touching you more deeply than others and want to concentrate on these for a while. Or you may find yourself focusing on images, memories and emotions — perhaps even sounds and fragrances — associated with the different parts of the reading.

Linger on any phrases or moments from the reading that touched you deeply, noticing the feelings evoked by them.

[3]   Now, ask God to guide you into this event in your imagination. Allow God to provide the words and actions that help place you in this moment with Jesus — whether becoming a part of the story or observing it. While you may refer to the biblical account during your prayer, do not be afraid if your imagination leads Jesus or other people in the episode to expand their conversation during your prayer — adding different words or phrases, perhaps mirroring your own speech patterns.

• Watch as Jesus and his disciples come into the garden, noting the particular appearances and actions of each — in relation to Jesus as well as to one another — as well as anything they carry with them. Look at Jesus as he speaks to his disciples before walking away from them to find a place to pray, observing any differences in mood or demeanor between Jesus and his disciples. Notice how their attitudes change after Jesus and his disciples are left alone.

• Take a moment to look around the garden, paying attention to how its trees and other plants are illuminated by the moonlight. See the place Jesus selects to pray, noting whether Jesus follows a path to it or walks across open ground. Look at Jesus as he prays, observing where he stands or sits as well as if Jesus can still see his disciples. Notice whether you feel warm or cool and whether you feel any wind on your skin.

• See and hear Jesus as he returns to his disciples during and after his prayers, noting the tone of his voice as he speaks with them each time he rejoins them. See Judas arrive with the party of armed soldiers, listening to the conversation between Jesus, Judas and the guards before seeing Jesus confront Simon Peter. Observe Jesus' actions and demeanor as he is arrested, noting the ways he interacts with Judas and the temple guards as well as his reaction when his disciples flee.

• See and hear Jesus as he is taken from the garden to the house of Annas, noticing how the behavior of each person in the group (including Jesus) changes when they enter the house. Listen to Annas as he questions Jesus, seeing the physical characteristics and mannerisms of the priest as well as his attitude toward Jesus. Observe Jesus responding to his questions and being struck by one of the guards before being taken from the house by the guards, noting who is in the house and how they react to Jesus as well as who goes with Jesus when he is sent to Caiaphas (as well as who remains behind).

As these images fade from your imagination, become aware of the emotions and memories that touched you most deeply — phrases or images, sounds or smells, etc. Make a mental note of any strong feelings evoked by these aspects of your prayer.

[4]   Then, see Jesus standing or sitting in front of you. Look at him — noting his physical characteristics and demeanor — as you become aware of your feelings as you are with him. Remember that Jesus wants to reveal himself to you, so try to be aware of his feelings toward you. Consider what you need to say to him about your recent prayer and open yourself to hear what he needs to say to you.

When you are ready, speak with Jesus as you would a close friend in an informal conversation. Allow your imagination to guide you freely as you speak, remaining open to changes in the topics of conversation and giving Jesus the space to introduce the issues and concerns from your recent prayer that he thinks are important for you to hear.

[5]   When you are ready, take a moment to gather any important thoughts, emotions and memories from this contemplation before concluding with this prayer from Alexander Carmichael's *Carmina Gadelica*:

O God of life, darken not to me your light,
O God of life, close not to me your joy,
O God of life, shut not to me your door,
    O God of life, refuse not to me your mercy,
    O God of life, quench toward me your wrath,
    O God of life, crown me with your gladness,
O God of life, crown me with your gladness. Amen.

[6]   Take 5-10 minutes to reflect on this time of prayer before recording your preliminary reflections in your journal.

A Contemplation of John 18 & 19

Chapter 18, Verse 28 through Chapter 19, Verse 16

[1]   Again, feel your desire to live in God's goodness so you may use the many gifts God has given you. Feeling God's continuing care to you, open yourself to the immense love God shows for you. Then, ask God to arouse in you deeper remorse and sorrow for your sins. Also, pray that you might share in Jesus' grief and brokenness during his Passion — as well as his deep sense of compassion, even for those that harmed him.

As these desires fill your consciousness, allow all other concerns to fall aside as you focus on this specific time and place.

[2]   Then, when you are ready, slowly read the account of Jesus' trial before Pontius Pilate in John 18: 28 through John 19: 16. As you read, you may find particular phrases from the passage touching you more deeply than others and want to concentrate on these for a while. Or you may find yourself focusing on images, memories and emotions — perhaps even sounds and fragrances — associated with the different parts of the reading.

Linger on any phrases or moments from the reading that touched you deeply, noticing the feelings evoked by them.

[3]   Now, ask God to guide you into this event in your imagination. Allow God to provide the words and actions that help place you in this moment with Jesus — whether becoming a part of the story or observing it. While you may refer to the biblical account during your prayer, do not be afraid if your imagination leads Jesus, Pontius Pilate or other people in the episode to expand their conversation during your prayer — adding different words or phrases, perhaps mirroring your own speech patterns.

• Watch as Jesus is taken before Pontius Pilate, noting the particular appearances and actions of each — toward one another and toward the assembled crowd. Listen to the conversation between Pilate and the priests, observing their actions and attitudes toward one another. Notice Jesus' physical appearance, actions and demeanor during this conversation.

• Take a moment to look at the buildings and open spaces around the Roman headquarters, paying attention to where the priests and their guards, the crowd and the Roman soldiers are standing in relation to Pilate and Jesus. Look at the place where Pontius Pilate and

Jesus are standing, noting its physical characteristics and its distance from the crowd. Watch as the crowd becomes increasingly hostile to Pilate and to Jesus, noticing the different ways this hostility affects Jesus and Pilate. Observe Pilate as he orders Jesus to be questioned inside the Roman garrison, noting the reaction of the priests and the crowd as Jesus is lead away.

• See and hear Jesus being questioned by Pilate, noting the words they say and how they act toward one another. Look around the room in which they speak, noticing who is there and what they are doing. Watch Pontius Pilate bring Jesus outside before addressing the crowd that has gathered, noting how Pilate tries to release Jesus and how he becomes fearful as his offer is rejected.

• See and hear Jesus being returned to the garrison — where he is flogged and mocked by the Roman soldiers — before being presented to the crowd, noticing how the cautious Pilate tries a second time to release Jesus. Watch the crowd become more insistent that Jesus be crucified, seeing and listening as Pilate again tries speaking to Jesus inside the garrison before returning with him to the courtyard. Observe Pilate as he condemns Jesus to death and orders his solders to crucify Jesus, noting the emotional responses in the crowd and among the priests as Jesus is taken away.

As these images fade from your imagination, become aware of the emotions and memories that touched you most deeply — phrases or images, sounds or smells, etc. Make a mental note of any strong feelings evoked by these aspects of your prayer.

[4]   Then, see Jesus standing or sitting in front of you. Look at him — noting his physical characteristics and demeanor — as you become aware of your feelings as you are with him. Remember that Jesus wants to reveal himself to you, so try to be aware of his feelings toward you. Consider what you need to say to him about your recent prayer and open yourself to hear what he needs to say to you.

When you are ready, speak with Jesus as you would a close friend in an informal conversation. Allow your imagination to guide you freely as you speak, remaining open to changes in the topics of conversation and giving Jesus the space to introduce the issues and concerns from your recent prayer that he thinks are important for you to hear.

[5]   When you are ready, take a moment to gather any important thoughts, emotions and memories from this contemplation before concluding with this prayer:

O God of life, darken not to me your light,
O God of life, close not to me your joy,
O God of life, shut not to me your door,
    O God of life, refuse not to me your mercy,
    O God of life, quench toward me your wrath,
    O God of life, crown me with your gladness,
O God of life, crown me with your gladness. Amen.

[6]   Again, take 5-10 minutes to reflect on this time of prayer before recording your preliminary reflections in your journal.

Verses 16 through 30

[1]   Again, feel your desire to live in God's goodness so you may use the many gifts God has given you. Feeling God's continuing care to you, open yourself to the immense love God shows for you. Then, ask God to arouse in you deeper remorse and sorrow for your sins. Also, pray that you might share in Jesus' grief and brokenness during his Passion — as well as his deep sense of compassion, even for those that harmed him.

As these desires fill your consciousness, allow all other concerns to fall aside as you focus on this specific time and place.

[2]   Then, when you are ready, slowly read the account of Jesus' death on the cross in John 19: 16-30. As you read, you may find particular phrases from the passage touching you more deeply than others and want to concentrate on these for a while. Or you may find yourself focusing on images, memories and emotions — perhaps even sounds and fragrances — associated with the different parts of the reading.

Linger on any phrases or moments from the reading that touched you deeply, noticing the feelings evoked by them.

[3]   Now, ask God to guide you into this event in your imagination. Allow God to provide the words and actions that help place you in this moment with Jesus — whether becoming a part of the story or observing it. While you may refer to the biblical account during your prayer, do not be afraid if your imagination leads Jesus or other people in the episode to expand their conversation during your prayer — adding different words or phrases, perhaps mirroring your own speech patterns.

• Watch Jesus carry his cross up the hill to be crucified, noting the physical characteristics of the cross and Jesus' actions as he carries it. Listen to the soldiers and crowd around Jesus as they walk beside him, hearing the different things that are said to Jesus as he goes to his death. Notice how he struggles under the weight of the cross but continues to demonstrate his strength of will and purpose.

• Take a moment to look around the place of crucifixion, paying attention to its physical characteristics and to where the crowd has gathered. Watch as Jesus is stripped before being tied and nailed to the cross, listening to him as the nails are hammered and the cross is lifted up from the ground. See the soldiers dividing his clothing among themselves, observing them as they gamble to decide who will receive his tunic. Notice the reactions of the priests when they see the inscription on the cross.

• See and hear as Jesus sees his mother, noting how he struggles to speak to her and to his disciple while also considering the feelings expressed in his words. Watch the response of Mary and the disciples near the cross as they listen to Jesus, seeing the various reactions of the crowd to this conversation. Observe Jesus as he weakens, noticing his actions and behavior as well as the actions of the crowd watching Jesus die.

• Hear Jesus say he is thirsty and see who offers him a sponge soaked in sour wine, noticing the reactions of the other people around Jesus — his mother, his disciples, the soldiers and the crowd. Watch and listen as Jesus dies on the cross, hearing his final words before his body becomes limp on the cross. Then, take a moment to look at his corpse and listen to the people as they respond to his death.

As these images fade from your imagination, become aware of the emotions and memories that touched you most deeply — phrases or images, sounds or smells, etc. Make a mental note of any strong feelings evoked by these aspects of your prayer.

[4] Then, see Jesus standing or sitting in front of you. Look at him — noting his physical characteristics and demeanor — as you become aware of your feelings as you are with him. Remember that Jesus wants to reveal himself to you, so try to be aware of his feelings toward you. Consider what you need to say to him about your recent prayer and open yourself to hear what he needs to say to you.

When you are ready, speak with Jesus as you would a close friend in an informal conversation. Allow your imagination to guide you freely as you speak, remaining open to changes in the topics of conversation and giving Jesus the space to introduce the issues and concerns from your recent prayer that he thinks are important for you to hear.

[5] When you are ready, take a moment to gather any important thoughts, emotions and memories from this contemplation before concluding with this prayer:

O God of life, darken not to me your light,
O God of life, close not to me your joy,
O God of life, shut not to me your door,
O God of life, refuse not to me your mercy,

O God of life, quench toward me your wrath,
O God of life, crown me with your gladness,
O God of life, crown me with your gladness. Amen.

[6]   Again, take 5-10 minutes to reflect on this time of prayer before recording your preliminary reflections in your journal.

A meditation on Psalm 22

Verses 1 through 11, continuing with Verses 23 through 31

[1]   Again, feel your desire to live in God's goodness so you may use the many gifts God has given you. Feeling God's continuing care to you, open yourself to the immense love God shows for you. Then, ask God to arouse in you deeper remorse and sorrow for your sins. Also, pray that you might share in Jesus' grief and brokenness during his Passion — as well as his deep sense of compassion, even for those that harmed him.

As these desires fill your consciousness, allow all other concerns to fall aside as you focus on this specific time and place.

[2]   Then, when you are ready, imagine meeting the suffering Judas with Brendan and his companions:

• Watch Brendan and his companions as they sail on the ocean, noting the actions and mood of the various travelers before they notice an unusual island on the horizon. Listen as the monks offer different opinions about an object on the island and what it might be, observing their various degrees of interest in knowing more about the object. Notice how Brendan prayerfully considers the object before instructing the monks to sail toward the object.

• Take a moment to look at the island as the monks approach it, paying attention to a man sitting on a barren rock with a small cloth suspended in front of him between two iron rods. Look at the man and see that the waves crash over him and the wind causes the cloth to hit his face, noting the reactions of the monks to this man's situation. Become aware of whether the day is sunny or cloudy as you look around the island and looking down into the water around it, observing any sea birds in the air and any fish in the ocean. Notice whether you feel heat or wind on your skin as well as whether you feel warm or cool.

• See and hear Brendan as he asks the man what he has done to deserve this punishment, noting his response when the man says that he is Judas and that this is actually a blessing. Listen to the conversation between Brendan and Judas, noticing Brendan's attitude and demeanor as Judas explains why he is sitting on the island and what the different objects around him represent. Observe Brendan as he promises Judas his protection, noting the different reactions of Judas and Brendan's

137

companions.

• See and hear the demons approaching the island, listening to the sound of their arrival and noticing their physical appearance and mannerisms when they ask Brendan to leave so they may torment Judas. Look at Brendan as he responds to the demons, noting his confidence as he challenges them and asserts God's authority over them and their master. Observe Brendan's various acts of kindness toward Judas, noting how this infuriates the demons during the night.

As the monks leave Judas' island in the morning, focus your attention on Brendan. See prayerfully guiding and reassuring his companions as the demons follow them, noting how the various monks respond to this encouragement from their abbot. Take a moment to notice the different reactions of Brendan and his companions as the demons leave them and return to Judas' island.

[3]   After the demons move beyond the horizon, hear Brendan instruct his companion monks to pray and ask God to help you join in their prayer — allowing you to join with the monks or to listen quietly while they pray.

Then, slowly read Psalm 22: 1-11, 23-31 while seeing and hearing Brendan and his companions chant the psalm in your imagination. You may find that particular phrases touch you more deeply than others. Or you may find specific images, memories and emotions — perhaps even sounds and fragrances — associated with the different parts of the psalm. Make a mental note of these things.

After the monks conclude their prayer, allow their image to fade from your imagination as you become aware of the particular phrases and images from the psalm which touched you most deeply. Recall the emotions and memories — as well as any sounds or smells — evoked by the words of the psalm. Allow these key aspects of your prayer to linger on your mind and in your heart, making a mental note of any special feelings evoked by them.

When you are ready, speak with God in an open and informal manner about how the psalm expresses your own needs or desires — giving space for God to respond or to highlight different aspects of the psalm. Gradually allow your thoughts to recede as you focus on God's presence in your life and in the world around you.

[4]   When you are ready, take a moment to gather any important thoughts, emotions and memories from this meditation before concluding with this prayer:

O God of life, darken not to me your light,

O God of life, close not to me your joy,
O God of life, shut not to me your door,
    O God of life, refuse not to me your mercy,
    O God of life, quench toward me your wrath,
    O God of life, crown me with your gladness,
O God of life, crown me with your gladness. Amen.

[5]   Again, take 5-10 minutes to reflect on this time of prayer before recording your preliminary reflections in your journal.

An Application of the Senses

[1]   Again, feel your desire to live in God's goodness so you may use the many gifts God has given you. Feel God's continuing care as you open yourself to the immense love God shows for you and ask God to arouse in you deeper remorse and sorrow for your sins. Also, pray that you might share in Jesus' grief and brokenness during his Passion — as well as his deep sense of compassion, even for those that harmed him.

Then, focus on this moment as all other concerns fade away.

[2]   When you are ready, using your imagination, call to mind the events as Saint Brendan meets Judas and challenges the demons. Allow the images and words of this story to linger and then slowly fade from your consciousness. Consider the images and feelings evoked in you during your prayer, feeling God's presence in these memories and becoming aware of the specific sensations associated with each image.

Then, in turn, remember your recent prayers on Psalm 22 and the Passion of Jesus. As these prayers enter your memory, make a mental note of which senses are most active. You may see an image or a color, hear a sound or a phrase, or smell a scent or a fragrance. You may even taste a flavor or feel a sensation on your skin.

Finally, relax and allow these various memories and experiences to quietly enter and leave your consciousness without being controlled — whether they are clear or diffuse, whether they come quickly or slowly. Linger on the sensory images and memories being evoked in you — noticing any images or colors, any sounds or phrases, any scents or fragrances, any flavors or physical sensations associated with each prayer.

[3]   When you are ready, become completely still and clear your mind of all thoughts and concerns. Watch as God forms a small image or object in your mind containing the most important gift you have been given during this particular time of prayer — the thought or awareness that you most need to carry with you into your life.

Reverently pick up the object or image, looking at it carefully and becoming aware of the divine presence contained within it. Take a moment to register what it looks like and how it feels in your hand. Then, feel the joy and confidence that comes from touching the presence of God as you accept this gift, offering a short prayer of gratitude while you relax into the pleasure of this moment.

[4]   Then, conclude by offering this prayer:
O God of life, darken not to me your light,
O God of life, close not to me your joy,
O God of life, shut not to me your door,
          O God of life, refuse not to me your mercy,
          O God of life, quench toward me your wrath,
          O God of life, crown me with your gladness,
O God of life, crown me with your gladness. Amen.
[5]   While your experiences are still fresh in your mind, record the most significant impressions or sensations from this time of prayer in your journal and thank God for the special gift you received from him.

Review

[1] Remember your desire that God arouse in you deeper remorse and sorrow for your sins. Recall how you asked that you might share in Jesus' grief and brokenness during his Passion — as well as his deep sense of compassion, even for those that harmed him. Then, take a moment to allow the words, thoughts and feelings from your prayers during the last day or week to linger — on your mind and in your heart — before asking God to reveal His presence in these various memories.

[2] Think about the events as Saint Brendan meets Judas and challenges the demons. Remember the parts of the story that spoke most powerfully to you and think about how elements of this story resurfaced in your recent prayers on Psalm 22 and Jesus' Passion. Ask God to help you understand these moments.

[3] Consider your meditations on Psalm 22. Recall the most powerful images, phrases or feelings from your prayer. Ask yourself what gifts God gave to you through these moments, perhaps offering you new insights or perhaps affirming an important aspect of your faith. Ask yourself how God may be calling you to change through these moments, being as specific as possible.

Examine your disposition as you prayed, noting whether prayer came easily or with resistance. Recall the easiest moments in your prayer and any moments of joy you may have experienced. Remember also if you encountered any difficulty opening yourself to God or if you felt any sadness as you prayed. Ask God to help you understand why these feelings surfaced.

Bring to mind any moments when you added personal elements — familiar places or people from your life — or connected your prayers to other scriptures or spiritual writings. Ask yourself how these additions helped or hindered you as you prayed. Again, if you do not know why this happened, ask God to help you understand.

[4] Ponder your contemplation of Jesus's Passion, allowing a mental picture of these events to form in your mind as you recall the perspective from which you experienced them. Then, review your prayer in the same way as your earlier reflection on Psalm 22.

[5] Recall the ebb and flow of sensory impressions and feelings that marked your application of the senses. Isolate the most memorable moments and sensory impressions from your prayer and reflect on how God used these moments to give you a particular gift, perhaps offering

you new insights or changing you in some way. Then, consider what you want to offer God in return for these moments.

[6]   Finally, remember the times when images or feelings from the readings of this day or week surfaced outside these prayer periods. Consider those moments or events in which God's presence or guidance was especially strong as well as any moments when you were struggling. Think about the most memorable aspects of these experiences, asking God to explain their significance.

[7]   Take a moment to allow the words, thoughts and feelings of these prayers to linger on your mind and in your heart. Then, conclude by asking for God's continued presence and guidance as you offer this prayer:

> *Bless to me, O God,*
> > *Each thing my eyes see;*
> *Bless to me, O God,*
> > *Each sound my ears hear;*
> *Bless to me, O God,*
> > *Each odor that goes to my nostrils;*
> *Bless to me, O God,*
> > *Each taste that goes to my lips;*
> > *Each note that goes to my song,*
> > *Each ray that guides my way,*
> > *Each thing that I pursue,*
> > *Each lure that tempts my will,*
> > *The zeal that seeks my living soul,*
> > *The Three that seek my heart,*
> > *The zeal that seeks my living soul,*
> > *The Three that seek my heart. Amen.*

[8]   After finishing these prayers, summarize the most significant moments, insights or desires from this last day or week in your journal before concluding these reflections in a short prayer of gratitude for the specific gifts or graces received during your prayers.

VIII • THE ISLAND OF PAUL THE HERMIT

Preparation

Consideration of the Readings:

After attending or prayerfully reading the prayer service for this day or week:

• Read (or hear) "The Island of Paul the Hermit" and its companion reflection, "Welcoming Others into the Resurrection". Allow yourself to linger on any thoughts or phrases that seem particularly meaningful or relevant to your life. Then, record these moments in your workbook.

• Read Psalm 91. Again, pay careful attention to any phrases or images that seem particularly meaningful to you. Then, record these highlights from the psalm in your workbook so you will remember them during the meditations on these readings in this section of the retreat.

• Read the resurrection accounts in John 20: 1-29. Make a mental note of each person's appearance and actions during the episode as well as the key elements of the story, including the setting. Again, record in your workbook any aspects of this story that speak strongly to you.

• Finally, read John 15: 1-12. Allow your thoughts to linger on phrases or images that seem germane to your life or experience before recording these reflections in your workbook.

Note: You also should take a moment to consider any aspect of the prayer service from this day or week that seemed particularly significant to you.

Contemplation of Your Needs:

When you are ready, concentrating on your breath or an object near you, allow any distractions to fade from your consciousness as you become aware of your desire to live in God's goodness. Feel yourself yearning to properly use the many gifts God has given you, to experience God's continuing care, and to be open to the immense love God shows for you.

Then, pray for your desires in the coming day or week. Ask God to awaken your heart to gladness so you may rejoice in the glory of the Risen Lord. Also, pray that you might see Jesus with new eyes as you follow him with renewed confidence and devotion in the assurance of

Christ's resurrection. Allow these desires to linger on your mind and in your heart for a few moments before slowly reviewing your notes on the readings for the coming day or week, asking God to be with you during these prayers — giving you the spiritual gifts you need from each of these readings as well as in your life after the retreat.

Finally, put your notes aside. Without straining your memory, consider in turn each of the readings for the coming day or week and allow them to take shape in your imagination — even if all you remember are small fragments. Prayerfully ponder how each reading affects you emotionally without overtly thinking about their content, asking God to illuminate the spiritual gifts offered in each reading — quieting your mind and creating a receptive space in yourself to see or hear the response.

Then, conclude by allowing these desires to fade from your consciousness as you offer this traditional prayer from Alexander Carmichael's *Carmina Gadelica*:

> Bless to me, O God,
>> Each thing my eyes see;
> Bless to me, O God,
>> Each sound my ears hear;
> Bless to me, O God,
>> Each odor that goes to my nostrils;
> Bless to me, O God,
>> Each taste that goes to my lips;
>> Each note that goes to my song,
>> Each ray that guides my way,
>> Each thing that I pursue,
>> Each lure that tempts my will,
>> The zeal that seeks my living soul,
> The Three that seek my heart,
>> The zeal that seeks my living soul,
> The Three that seek my heart. Amen.

Allow these words to linger on your mind and in your heart for a few moments and then, while they are still fresh in your memory, write the most important thoughts and feelings from this preparatory prayer in your workbook or journal.

<u>Note:</u> *Remember to allow the dynamics of this preparation to guide you into the later prayers in this section of your retreat.*

A Contemplation of John 20

Verses 1 through 18

[1]   Become aware of your desire to live in God's goodness so you may use the many gifts God has given you. Feel God's continuing care for you and open yourself to the immense love God shows for you. Then, ask God to awaken your heart to gladness so you may rejoice in the glory of the Risen Lord. Also, pray that you might see Jesus with new eyes as you follow him with renewed confidence and devotion in the assurance of Christ's resurrection.

As these desires fill your consciousness, allow all other concerns to fall aside as you focus on this specific time and place.

[2]   Then, when you are ready, slowly read the account of the appearance of the Risen Jesus to Mary Magdalene in John 20: 1-18. As you read, you may find particular phrases from the passage touching you more deeply than others and want to concentrate on these for a while. Or you may find yourself focusing on images, memories and emotions — perhaps even sounds and fragrances — associated with the different parts of the reading.

Linger on any phrases or moments from the reading that touched you deeply, noticing the feelings evoked by them.

[3]   Now, ask God to guide you into this event in your imagination. Allow God to provide the words and actions that help place you in this moment with Jesus — whether becoming a part of the story or observing it. While you may refer to the biblical account during your prayer, do not be afraid if your imagination leads Jesus, Mary Magdalene or the disciples to expand their conversation during your prayer — adding different words or phrases, perhaps mirroring your own speech patterns.

• Watch Mary Magdalene approaching Jesus' tomb in the darkness, looking at her physical characteristics and clothing as well as seeing what she carries to light her way. Observe her reaction when she sees that the stone has been removed from its entrance, noting how close she comes to the tomb before realizing that the tomb is empty. Notice any changes in her posture and demeanor from when she first approached the tomb and when she runs to tell Simon Peter that Jesus' body has been removed.

• Take a moment to look at the tomb and the area around it, paying attention to the terrain around it and whether the tomb stands

146

alone or surrounded by other tombs. Look at the tomb's cover stone, noting its physical characteristics and location in relation to the tomb's entrance. Listen for any animals making sounds in the early morning and look at the trees and other vegetation around the tomb, noting whether you feel heat or wind on your skin as the sun begins to rise. Notice your own feelings as you look at the empty tomb.

• See and hear Simon Peter and another disciple run toward the open tomb, noting that the first disciple arrives first but waits at the entrance before Simon Peter arrives and enters it. Watch their appearance and actions of these two men and see their reactions when they see Jesus' death wrappings in the tomb, listening to their conversation and hearing their reactions to this situation. Observe Mary Magdalene as she returns to the tomb and tries to speak with Simon Peter and the other disciple, noting her reaction when they leave her alone at the tomb.

• See and hear Mary as she weeps at the entrance to the tomb after the other disciples leave, noticing her reaction as she cautiously looks into the tomb and sees two angels sitting in it. Listen to her conversation with the angels, hearing the insistence as she asks them to tell her the location of Jesus' body. Observe her actions as turns away from the tomb and speaks with the stranger standing near her, noting her response when she recognizes the Risen Jesus and then watching her leave to tell the other disciples what she has seen.

As this image fades from your imagination become aware of the emotions and memories that touched you most deeply — phrases or images, sounds or smells, etc. Make a mental note of any strong feelings evoked by these aspects of your prayer.

[4]   Then, see Jesus standing or sitting in front of you. Look at him — noting his physical characteristics and demeanor — as you become aware of your feelings as you are with him. Remember that Jesus wants to reveal himself to you, so try to be aware of his feelings toward you. Consider what you need to say to him about your recent prayer and open yourself to hear what he needs to say to you.

When you are ready, speak with Jesus as you would a close friend in an informal conversation. Allow your imagination to guide you freely as you speak, remaining open to changes in the topics of conversation and giving Jesus the space to introduce the issues and concerns from your recent prayer that he thinks are important for you to hear.

[5]   When you are ready, take a moment to gather any important

thoughts, emotions and memories from this contemplation before concluding with this prayer from Alexander Carmichael's *Carmina Gadelica*:

> *O God of life, darken not to me your light,*
> *O God of life, close not to me your joy,*
> *O God of life, shut not to me your door,*
> > *O God of life, refuse not to me your mercy,*
> > *O God of life, quench toward me your wrath,*
> > *O God of life, crown me with your gladness,*
> *O God of life, crown me with your gladness. Amen.*

[6]   Take 5-10 minutes to reflect on this time of prayer before recording your preliminary reflections in your journal.

A meditation on Psalm 91

Verses 1 through 16

[1]   Again, feel your desire to live in God's goodness so you may use the many gifts God has given you. Feeling God's continuing care to you, open yourself to the immense love God shows for you. Then, ask God to awaken your heart to gladness so you may rejoice in the glory of the Risen Lord. Also, pray that you might see Jesus with new eyes as you follow him with renewed confidence and devotion in the assurance of Christ's resurrection.

As these desires fill your consciousness, allow all other concerns to fall aside as you focus on this specific time and place.

[2]   Then, when you are ready, imagine visiting Paul the Hermit with Brendan and his companions.

• Watch Brendan and his companions struggle to land on a small island, noting the high cliffs and rocky terrain of the small circular island. Look at the monks, seeing they are tired and nearing exhaustion and hearing Brendan tells them that they will rest on this island and meet Paul the Hermit. Notice the various reactions of the monks when finally find a small landing spot but Brendan tells them to remain in the boat until they receive permission to step ashore.

• Take a moment to watch Brendan climb to the top of the island, paying attention to his actions and demeanor as he looks at the entrances to two caves facing one another and a small spring between them. Watch the water suddenly flow up from the spring before being absorbed by the rocks once again, noting Brendan's reaction to the gentle action of the water. Then, look at the sky and become aware of whether the day is sunny or cloudy, becoming aware of whether the air feels humid or dry. Notice whether you feel heat or wind on your skin as well as whether you feel warm or cool.

• See and hear Paul the Hermit come out of his cave to greet Brendan, noting that the naked hermit is covered entirely by his long white hair and beard. Listen to Paul as he asks Brendan to invite his companions ashore, noticing his physical actions and mannerisms as he welcomes each monk by name. Observe the reactions of the different monks to this holy hermit, noting how Paul treats each monk as a unique individual while speaking of their shared brotherhood.

• See and hear Brendan express his admiration for Paul and his spiritual heroism, noticing how Paul reminds Brendan of the unique spiritual gifts received through his own journey. Listen as the hermit tells Brendan and his companions the story of his own journey to this island and the ways in which God has sustained him in the years since he arrived, seeing the various reactions of the visiting monks to his story. Observe Paul as he invites the monks to take some of the water from his well to nourish them on their travels, watching the monks leave briefly before returning to fill various vessels with water from the well.

As the monks fill their vessels with water, focus your attention on Brendan. See where he is sitting, noting his physical appearance and emotional demeanor as he contemplates Paul's story and situation. Take a moment to notice whether this make him happy or melancholy.

[3]   As Paul invites Brendan and his companions to pray with him in gratitude for their safe arrival on his island, ask God to help you join in their prayer — allowing you to join with the monks or to listen quietly while they pray.

Then, slowly read Psalm 91: 1-16 while seeing and hearing Paul and his visitors chant the psalm in your imagination. You may find that particular phrases touch you more deeply than others. Or you may find specific images, memories and emotions — perhaps even sounds and fragrances — associated with the different parts of the psalm. Make a mental note of these things.

After the monks conclude their prayer, allow their image to fade from your imagination as you become aware of the particular phrases and images from the psalm which touched you most deeply. Recall the emotions and memories — as well as any sounds or smells — evoked by the words of the psalm. Allow these key aspects of your prayer to linger on your mind and in your heart, making a mental note of any special feelings evoked by them.

When you are ready, speak with God in an open and informal manner about how the psalm expresses your own needs or desires — giving space for God to respond or to highlight different aspects of the psalm. Gradually allow your thoughts to recede as you focus on God's presence in your life and in the world around you.

[4]   When you are ready, take a moment to gather any important thoughts, emotions and memories from this meditation before concluding with this prayer:

O God of life, darken not to me your light,
O God of life, close not to me your joy,
O God of life, shut not to me your door,

O God of life, refuse not to me your mercy,
O God of life, quench toward me your wrath,
O God of life, crown me with your gladness,
O God of life, crown me with your gladness. Amen.

[5]   Again, take 5-10 minutes to reflect on this time of prayer before recording your preliminary reflections in your journal.

Verses 19 through 29

[1]	Again, feel your desire to live in God's goodness so you may use the many gifts God has given you. Feeling God's continuing care to you, open yourself to the immense love God shows for you. Then, ask God to awaken your heart to gladness so you may rejoice in the glory of the Risen Lord. Also, pray that you might see Jesus with new eyes as you follow him with renewed confidence and devotion in the assurance of Christ's resurrection.

As these desires fill your consciousness, allow all other concerns to fall aside as you focus on this specific time and place.

[2]	Then, when you are ready, slowly read the account of the appearances of the Risen Jesus to his disciples in John 20: 19-29. As you read, you may find particular phrases from the passage touching you more deeply than others and want to concentrate on these for a while. Or you may find yourself focusing on images, memories and emotions — perhaps even sounds and fragrances — associated with the different parts of the reading.

Linger on any phrases or moments from the reading that touched you deeply, noticing the feelings evoked by them.

[3]	Now, ask God to guide you into this event in your imagination. Allow God to provide the words and actions that help place you in this moment with Jesus — whether becoming a part of the story or observing it. While you may refer to the biblical account during your prayer, do not be afraid if your imagination leads Jesus or the disciples to expand their conversation during your prayer — adding different words or phrases, perhaps mirroring your own speech patterns.

• Watch the disciples locked in a room at evening time, noticing the physical appearance and particular actions and attitudes of each person. See Jesus appear in the room, noting his physical appearance and attitude towards the disciples as he offers his greeting of peace. Notice the various reactions of the different disciples to Jesus' appearance.

• Take a moment to look around the room, paying attention to its physical characteristics — its size and shape as well as the location of its doors and windows. See the furniture and decorations in the room, noting the shape and construction of these objects as well as their location. Look at the light sources, noting where they are located and whether the lighting is bright or muted. Notice whether the room feels humid or dry as well as whether it feels warm or cool on your skin.

• See and hear Jesus speaking with his disciples before breathing on them and giving them the Holy Spirit, noting the different reactions of the various disciples to Jesus' words and actions. Listen as Jesus speaks with each disciple, hearing the compassion in his voice and noticing the various responses from the different disciples to the Risen Jesus' presence. Observe Thomas' arrival after Jesus has left and listen to the conversation between him and other the disciples, hearing Thomas challenge his companions and noting their responses.

• See and hear Jesus appear to the disciples again, listening as Jesus speaks with Thomas and demands that he touch his wounds. Listen to the tone of Jesus' voice as he speaks, seeing how it affects Thomas as he steps toward the Risen Jesus. Observe Thomas as he places his fingers in Jesus' hands and places his hand in Jesus' side, noting Thomas' physical and emotional response to his own actions and hearing Jesus' words to Thomas and the other disciples before he disappears.

As this image fades from your imagination become aware of the emotions and memories that touched you most deeply — phrases or images, sounds or smells, etc. Make a mental note of any strong feelings evoked by these aspects of your prayer.

[4]   Then, see Jesus standing or sitting in front of you. Look at him — noting his physical characteristics and demeanor — as you become aware of your feelings as you are with him. Remember that Jesus wants to reveal himself to you, so try to be aware of his feelings toward you. Consider what you need to say to him about your recent prayer and open yourself to hear what he needs to say to you.

When you are ready, speak with Jesus as you would a close friend in an informal conversation. Allow your imagination to guide you freely as you speak, remaining open to changes in the topics of conversation and giving Jesus the space to introduce the issues and concerns from your recent prayer that he thinks are important for you to hear.

[5]   When you are ready, take a moment to gather any important thoughts, emotions and memories from this contemplation before concluding with this prayer:

O God of life, darken not to me your light,
O God of life, close not to me your joy,

O God of life, shut not to me your door,
    O God of life, refuse not to me your mercy,
    O God of life, quench toward me your wrath,
    O God of life, crown me with your gladness,
O God of life, crown me with your gladness. Amen.

[6]   Again, take 5-10 minutes to reflect on this time of prayer before recording your preliminary reflections in your journal.

A consideration of John 15

Verses 1 through 12

[1]   Again, feel your desire to live in God's goodness so you may use the many gifts God has given you. Feeling God's continuing care to you, open yourself to the immense love God shows for you. Then, ask God to awaken your heart to gladness so you may rejoice in the glory of the Risen Lord. Also, pray that you might see Jesus with new eyes as you follow him with renewed confidence and devotion in the assurance of Christ's resurrection.

As these desires fill your consciousness, allow all other concerns to fall aside as you focus on this specific time and place.

[2]   Then, take a moment to ponder the transformative power of Christ's resurrection — bringing life out of death, joy out of pain — and consider the places in the world that most need to experience the presence of the Risen Christ. Allow images of these various locations to ebb and flow in your consciousness, looking for signs of Christ's presence in the work of those working to improve these situations and in the lives of the people living there.

In your imagination, see a place where you have experienced the power of Christ's resurrection in your own life. Look around you, noticing the physical characteristics of this place. Carefully observe any people living there, seeing each as a unique child of God and listening to these people speaking about their joys and their sorrows. Consider any feelings evoked in you while you are in this place.

Imagine Jesus approaching you. Greet him and allow him to welcome you into this place of his resurrection. Ask him where he lives in this place and allow him to show you.   Then, either walking or sitting with him, hear him tell you the allegory of the vine as you read John 15: 1-12. Afterward, speak with him about this allegory and its significance for you in this particular place.

[3]   After your conversation concludes, allow the image of Jesus to fade slowly from your consciousness. Feel the residue of consolation that remains after being with a close and dear friend as you conclude by offering this prayer:

> O God of life, darken not to me your light,
> O God of life, close not to me your joy,
> O God of life, shut not to me your door,
>   O God of life, refuse not to me your mercy,

O God of life, quench toward me your wrath,
O God of life, crown me with your gladness,
O God of life, crown me with your gladness. Amen.

[4]   Again, take 5-10 minutes to reflect on this time of prayer before recording your preliminary reflections in your journal.

An Application of the Senses

[1]   Again, feel your desire to live in God's goodness so you may use the many gifts God has given you. Feel God's continuing care as you open yourself to the immense love God shows for you and ask God to awaken your heart to gladness so you may rejoice in the glory of the Risen Lord. Also, pray that you might see Jesus with new eyes as you follow him with renewed confidence and devotion in the assurance of Christ's resurrection.

Then, focus on this moment as all other concerns fade away.

[2]   When you are ready, using your imagination, remember the various events during Brendan's visit with Paul the Hermit. Allow the images and words of this story to linger and then slowly fade from your consciousness. Consider the images and feelings evoked in you during your prayer, feeling God's presence in these memories and becoming aware of the specific sensations associated with each image.

Then, in turn, remember your recent prayers on Psalm 91, the appearances of the Risen Jesus in John 20, and your conversation with Jesus about John 15. As these prayers enter your memory, make a mental note of which senses are most active. You may see an image or a color, hear a sound or a phrase, or smell a scent or a fragrance. You may even taste a flavor or feel a sensation on your skin.

Finally, relax and allow these various memories and experiences to quietly enter and leave your consciousness without being controlled — whether they are clear or diffuse, whether they come quickly or slowly. Linger on the sensory images and memories being evoked in you — noticing any images or colors, any sounds or phrases, any scents or fragrances, any flavors or physical sensations associated with each prayer.

[3]   When you are ready, become completely still and clear your mind of all thoughts and concerns. Watch as God forms a small image or object in your mind containing the most important gift you have been given during this particular time of prayer — the thought or awareness that you most need to carry with you into your life.

Reverently pick up the object or image, looking at it carefully and becoming aware of the divine presence contained within it. Take a moment to register what it looks like and how it feels in your hand. Then, feel the joy and confidence that comes from touching the presence of God as you accept this gift, offering a short prayer of gratitude while you relax into the pleasure of this moment.

[4]   Then, conclude by offering this prayer:

O God of life, darken not to me your light,
O God of life, close not to me your joy,
O God of life, shut not to me your door,
>   *O God of life, refuse not to me your mercy,*
>   *O God of life, quench toward me your wrath,*
>   *O God of life, crown me with your gladness,*
O God of life, crown me with your gladness. Amen.

[5]   While your experiences are still fresh in your mind, record the most significant impressions or sensations from this time of prayer in your journal and thank God for the special gift you received from him.

Review

[1]   Remember your desire to rejoice in the glory of the Risen Lord. Recall how you asked that you might see Jesus with new eyes as you follow him with renewed confidence and devotion in the assurance of Christ's resurrection. Then, take a moment to allow the words, thoughts and feelings from your prayers during the last day or week to linger — on your mind and in your heart — before asking God to reveal His presence in these various memories.

[2]   Think about Brendan's meeting with Paul the Hermit. Remember the parts of the story that spoke most powerfully to you and think about how elements of this story resurfaced in your recent prayers on Psalm 91, the appearances of the Risen Jesus to his disciples, and your conversation with Jesus about John 15. Ask God to help you understand these moments.

[3]   Consider your meditations on Psalm 91. Recall the most powerful images, phrases or feelings from your prayer. Ask yourself what gifts God gave to you through these moments, perhaps offering you new insights or perhaps affirming an important aspect of your faith. Ask yourself how God may be calling you to change through these moments, being as specific as possible.

Examine your disposition as you prayed, noting whether prayer came easily or with resistance. Recall the easiest moments in your prayer and any moments of joy you may have experienced. Remember also if you encountered any difficulty opening yourself to God or if you felt any sadness as you prayed. Ask God to help you understand why these feelings surfaced.

Bring to mind any moments when you added personal elements — familiar places or people from your life — or connected your prayers to other scriptures or spiritual writings. Ask yourself how these additions helped or hindered you as you prayed. Again, if you do not know why this happened, ask God to help you understand.

[4]   Ponder your contemplation of the appearances of the Risen Jesus in John 20, allowing a mental picture of these events to form in your mind as you recall the perspective from which you experienced them. Then, review your prayer in the same way as your earlier reflection on Psalm 91.

[5]   Review your conversation with Jesus as you discussed John 15: 1-12. Again, allow a mental picture of this imaginative contemplation

to form in your mind as you recall the details of this dialogue. Then, ponder your prayer in the same way as the earlier meditations on Psalm 91 and John 20.

[6]   Recall the ebb and flow of sensory impressions and feelings that marked your application of the senses. Isolate the most memorable moments and sensory impressions from your prayer and reflect on how God used these moments to give you a particular gift, perhaps offering you new insights or changing you in some way. Then, consider what you want to offer God in return for these moments.

[7]   Finally, remember the times when images or feelings from the readings of this day or week surfaced outside these prayer periods. Consider those moments or events in which God's presence or guidance was especially strong as well as any moments when you were struggling. Think about the most memorable aspects of these experiences, asking God to explain their significance.

[8]   Take a moment to allow the words, thoughts and feelings of these prayers to linger on your mind and in your heart. Then, conclude by asking for God's continued presence and guidance as you offer this prayer:

> Bless to me, O God,
>   Each thing my eyes see;
> Bless to me, O God,
>   Each sound my ears hear;
> Bless to me, O God,
>   Each odor that goes to my nostrils;
> Bless to me, O God,
>   Each taste that goes to my lips;
>   Each note that goes to my song,
>   Each ray that guides my way,
>   Each thing that I pursue,
>   Each lure that tempts my will,
>   The zeal that seeks my living soul,
>   The Three that seek my heart,
>   The zeal that seeks my living soul,
>   The Three that seek my heart. Amen.

[9]   After finishing these prayers, summarize the most significant moments, insights or desires from this last day or week in your journal before concluding these reflections in a short prayer of gratitude for the specific gifts or graces received during your prayers.

IX • THE PROMISED LAND OF THE SAINTS & THE RETURN HOME

Preparation

<u>Consideration of the Readings:</u>
> After attending or prayerfully reading the prayer service for this day or week:

> • Read (or hear) "The Promised Land of the Saints & The Return Home" and its companion reflection, "Treasuring the Gifts of Pilgrimage". Allow yourself to linger on any thoughts or phrases that seem particularly meaningful or relevant to your life. Then, record these moments in your workbook.

> • Read Psalm 116. Again, pay careful attention to any phrases or images that seem particularly meaningful to you. Then, record these highlights from the psalm in your workbook so you will remember them during the meditations on these readings in this section of the retreat.

> • Read the resurrection account in John 21: 1-14. Make a mental note of each person's appearance and actions during the episode as well as the key elements of the story, including the setting. Again, record in your workbook any aspects of this story that speak strongly to you.

> • Finally, re-read John 15: 1-12. Again, allow your thoughts to linger on phrases or images that seem germane to your life or experience before recording these reflections in your workbook.

> <u>Note:</u> *You also should take a moment to consider any aspect of the prayer service from this day or week that seemed particularly significant to you.*

<u>Consideration of Your Retreat</u>
> As your retreat approaches its end, you should resist the temptation to review your experiences too early. So, remain focused on the prayers of this section — and open to the specific graces God offers through them — by not treating them as part of the "finish line" for the spiritual journey you have been making with Brendan and his companions.

> Still, you will need to take a moment to set aside a time after your review of your prayers in this section (and before you end your retreat) to complete the exercise in the retreat's conclusion, devoting

half of the time you normally pray during the retreat. Avoid reading or considering the exercise until you are ready to do it, treating it as a special moment within your retreat that you approach without any presuppositions.

Contemplation of Your Needs:

When you are ready, concentrating on your breath or an object near you, allow any distractions to fade from your consciousness as you become aware of your desire to live in God's goodness. Feel yourself yearning to properly use the many gifts God has given you, to experience God's continuing care, and to be open to the immense love God shows for you.

Then, pray for your desires in the coming day or week. Ask God to grant you the gift of joy as you continue to walk in the presence of the Risen Christ through prayer and through service to others — whether in familiar circumstances or in those that require you to venture into the unknown. Allow these desires to linger on your mind and in your heart for a few moments before slowly reviewing your notes on the readings for the coming day or week, asking God to be with you during these prayers — giving you the spiritual gifts you need from each of these readings as well as in your life after the retreat.

Finally, put your notes aside. Without straining your memory, consider in turn each of the readings for the coming day or week and allow them to take shape in your imagination — even if all you remember are small fragments. Prayerfully ponder how each reading affects you emotionally without overtly thinking about their content, asking God to illuminate the spiritual gifts offered in each reading — quieting your mind and creating a receptive space in yourself to see or hear the response.

Then, conclude by allowing these desires to fade from your consciousness as you offer this traditional prayer from Alexander Carmichael's *Carmina Gadelica*:

Bless to me, O God,
    Each thing my eyes see;
Bless to me, O God,
    Each sound my ears hear;
Bless to me, O God,
    Each odor that goes to my nostrils;
Bless to me, O God,
    Each taste that goes to my lips;

Each note that goes to my song,
Each ray that guides my way,
Each thing that I pursue,
Each lure that tempts my will,
The zeal that seeks my living soul,
The Three that seek my heart,
The zeal that seeks my living soul,
The Three that seek my heart. Amen.

Allow these words to linger on your mind and in your heart for a few moments and then, while they are still fresh in your memory, write the most important thoughts and feelings from this preparatory prayer in your workbook or journal.

Note: *Remember to allow the dynamics of this preparation to guide you into the later prayers in this section of your retreat.*

Verses 1 through 9

[1]   Become aware of your desire to live in God's goodness so you may use the many gifts God has given you. Feel God's continuing care for you and open yourself to the immense love God shows for you. Then, ask God to grant you the gift of joy as you continue to walk in the presence of the Risen Christ through prayer and through service to others — whether in familiar circumstances or in those that require you to venture into the unknown.

As these desires fill your consciousness, allow all other concerns to fall aside as you focus on this specific time and place.

[2]   Then, when you are ready, imagine Brendan and his companions as they near the end of their journey.

• Watch Brendan and his companions leave the island of Paul the Hermit, noting their joy at being told they are nearing the end of their pilgrimage. Look at the monks as they return to the Island of Sheep, observing the welcome they receive from the steward who had helped them during their previous visit. Notice the confidence of the group as they meet and ride Jasconius to the Paradise of Birds.

• Take a moment to listen to the sound of the birds as Brendan and his companions leave their island, paying attention to how the steward guides them into a heavy fog. Hear the steward telling Brendan that he has almost reached his destination, watching their reactions as the boat emerges from the fog to reveal a beautiful island. Look at the island, noticing the details of its terrain and feeling a warm breeze touch your skin. Notice the brightness of the light on the island as you watch Brendan and his companions come ashore, noting their reactions to arriving at the place they had sought for so long.

• See and hear Brendan and his companions explore the island, noting their awe as they see that it is full of ripe fruit, flowering plants and precious gems. Watch the monks come to a large river, noticing their reactions as a young man appears and welcomes each of them by name. Listen as he explains that they cannot cross the river and must now return home — bringing whatever treasures they may carry in their boat — and observe the monks as they load their boat and leave the island. Notice the things that each member of the group — including Brendan — chooses to bring with them as they return home.

• See and hear Brendan and his companions as they sail

through the fog, noticing their emotional and spiritual demeanor as they prepare to return home. See them while they sail homeward, listening to their conversations as they meet various people along the way — on the Island of Delights and on the road to Clonfert after returning to Ireland. Observe the welcome they receive as they return to their home monastery, noting how Brendan and each of his companions respond to being home.

• As the monks are guided into the monastic enclosure, focus your attention on Brendan. See how he responds to each person he meets, noting how he warmly embraces his community members while remaining detached from their celebration. Take a moment to notice how his disposition changes each time a person welcomes him home.

[3]   As Brendan invites his monastic community to pray with him in gratitude for the gifts of their journey, ask God to help you join in their prayer — allowing you to join with the monks or to listen quietly while they pray.

Then, slowly read Psalm 116: 1-9 while seeing and hearing Brendan and his companions chant the psalm in your imagination. You may find that particular phrases touch you more deeply than others. Or you may find specific images, memories and emotions — perhaps even sounds and fragrances — associated with the different parts of the psalm. Make a mental note of these things.

After the monks conclude their prayer, allow their image to fade from your imagination as you become aware of the particular phrases and images from the psalm which touched you most deeply. Recall the emotions and memories — as well as any sounds or smells — evoked by the words of the psalm. Allow these key aspects of your prayer to linger on your mind and in your heart, making a mental note of any special feelings evoked by them.

When you are ready, speak with God in an open and informal manner about how the psalm expresses your own needs or desires — giving space for God to respond or to highlight different aspects of the psalm. Gradually allow your thoughts to recede as you focus on God's presence in your life and in the world around you.

[4]   When you are ready, take a moment to gather any important thoughts, emotions and memories from this meditation before concluding with this prayer from Alexander Carmichael's *Carmina Gadelica*:

> *O God of life, darken not to me your light,*
> *O God of life, close not to me your joy,*

165

O God of life, shut not to me your door,
      O God of life, refuse not to me your mercy,
      O God of life, quench toward me your wrath,
      O God of life, crown me with your gladness,
O God of life, crown me with your gladness. Amen.

[5]   Take 5-10 minutes to reflect on this time of prayer before recording your preliminary reflections in your journal.

A Contemplation of John 21

Verses 1 through 14

[1]   Again, feel your desire to live in God's goodness so you may use the many gifts God has given you. Feeling God's continuing care to you, open yourself to the immense love God shows for you. Then, ask God to grant you the gift of joy as you continue to walk in the presence of the Risen Christ through prayer and through service to others — whether in familiar circumstances or in those that require you to venture into the unknown.

As these desires fill your consciousness, allow all other concerns to fall aside as you focus on this specific time and place.

[2]   Then, when you are ready, slowly read the account of Jesus' appearance to his disciples on the shores of Lake Tiberias in John 21: 1-14. As you read, you may find particular phrases from the passage touching you more deeply than others and want to concentrate on these for a while. Or you may find yourself focusing on images, memories and emotions — perhaps even sounds and fragrances — associated with the different parts of the reading.

Linger any phrases or moments from the reading that touched you deeply, noticing the feelings evoked by them.

[3]   Now, ask God to guide you into this event in your imagination. Allow God to provide the words and actions that help place you in this moment with Jesus — whether becoming a part of the story or observing it. While you may refer to the biblical account during your prayer, do not be afraid if your imagination leads the Risen Jesus or his disciples to expand their conversation during your prayer — adding different words or phrases, perhaps mirroring your own speech patterns.

• Watch Simon Peter as he sits with the other disciples, noting his appearance and actions as well as how he seems distracted and irritable. Listen as he tells his companions that he will go fishing, hearing the responses from the other disciples and watching them follow him to the shore. Notice whether the disciples share Simon Peter's mood as they all get into the boat and set out onto the water.

• Take a moment to look at the boat, paying attention to its size and physical characteristics as well as how far above the water line it rides. See Simon Peter and his companions cast their nets into the water, feeling the cool air on your skin while listening to them talking as they repeatedly cast their nets but catch no fish. Hear the frustration and tiredness in their voices grow as they night wears on, observing the different attitudes expressed by each member of the group. Notice their response as they watch the sun begin to rise after the long night.

• See and hear a stranger address the disciples from the shore, hearing him tell the disciples to cast their nets on the other side of the boat. Watch the reactions of the various disciples when the net is suddenly full, noticing when and how Simon Peter recognizes Jesus. Observe that Simon Peter puts on some clothes before jumping into the water and swimming to the shore, noting the reactions of the other disciples as they are left to guide the boat back to shore.

• See and hear Jesus sitting with Simon Peter by a fire as the other disciples land the boat, noting what Jesus says to Simon Peter and how he greets the other disciples after they land the boat. Listen as Jesus tells Simon Peter to get some the fish from the boat, watching him pull the net ashore and return to Jesus. Observe Jesus as he invites the disciples to share breakfast with him, noting the behavior of the disciples toward Jesus and how none of them ask Jesus any questions as he offers them bread and fish to eat.

As this image fades from your imagination, become aware of the emotions and memories that touched you most deeply — phrases or images, sounds or smells, etc. Make a mental note of any strong feelings evoked by these aspects of your prayer.

[4]   Then, see Jesus standing or sitting in front of you. Look at him — noting his physical characteristics and demeanor — as you become aware of your feelings as you are with him. Remember that Jesus wants to reveal himself to you, so try to be aware of his feelings toward you. Consider what you need to say to him about your recent prayer and open yourself to hear what he needs to say to you.

When you are ready, speak with Jesus as you would a close friend in an informal conversation. Allow your imagination to guide you freely as you speak, remaining open to changes in the topics of conversation and giving Jesus the space to introduce the issues and concerns from your recent prayer that he thinks are important for you to hear.

[5]   When you are ready, take a moment to gather any important thoughts, emotions and memories from this contemplation before concluding with this prayer:

O God of life, darken not to me your light,
O God of life, close not to me your joy,

O God of life, shut not to me your door,
O God of life, refuse not to me your mercy,
O God of life, quench toward me your wrath,
O God of life, crown me with your gladness,
O God of life, crown me with your gladness. Amen.

[6]   Again, take 5-10 minutes to reflect on this time of prayer before recording your preliminary reflections in your journal.

Verses 1 through 19

[1]   Again, feel your desire to live in God's goodness so you may use the many gifts God has given you. Feeling God's continuing care to you, open yourself to the immense love God shows for you. Then, ask God to grant you the gift of joy as you continue to walk in the presence of the Risen Christ through prayer and through service to others — whether in familiar circumstances or in those that require you to venture into the unknown.

As these desires fill your consciousness, allow all other concerns to fall aside as you focus on this specific time and place.

[2]   Then, when you are ready, imagine Brendan and his companions as they near the end of their journey.

• Watch Brendan and his companions leave the island of Paul the Hermit, noting their joy at being told they are nearing the end of their pilgrimage. Look at the monks as they return to the Island of Sheep, observing the welcome they receive from the steward who had helped them during their previous visit. Notice the confidence of the group as they meet and ride Jasconius to the Paradise of Birds.

• Take a moment to listen to the sound of the birds as Brendan and his companions leave their island, paying attention to how the steward guides them into a heavy fog. Hear the steward telling Brendan that he has almost reached his destination, watching their reactions as the boat emerges from the fog to reveal a beautiful island. Look at the island, noticing the details of its terrain and feeling a warm breeze touch your skin. Notice the brightness of the light on the island as you watch Brendan and his companions come ashore, noting their reactions to arriving at the place they had sought for so long.

• See and hear Brendan and his companions explore the island, noting their awe as they see that it is full of ripe fruit, flowering plants and precious gems. Watch the monks come to a large river, noticing their reactions as a young man appears and welcomes each of them by name. Listen as he explains that they cannot cross the river and must now return home — bringing whatever treasures they may carry in their boat — and observe the monks as they load their boat and leave the island. Notice the things that each member of the group — including Brendan — chooses to bring with them as they return home.

• See and hear Brendan and his companions as they sail

through the fog, noticing their emotional and spiritual demeanor as they prepare to return home. See them while they sail homeward, listening to their conversations as they meet various people along the way — on the Island of Delights and on the road to Clonfert after returning to Ireland. Observe the welcome they receive as they return to their home monastery, noting how Brendan and each of his companions respond to being home.

• As the monks are guided into the monastic enclosure, focus your attention on Brendan. See how he responds to each person he meets, noting how he warmly embraces his community members while remaining detached from their celebration. Take a moment to notice how his disposition changes each time a person welcomes him home.

[3]   As Brendan invites his monastic community to pray with him in gratitude for the gifts of their journey, ask God to help you join in their prayer — allowing you to join with the monks or to listen quietly while they pray.

Then, slowly read Psalm 116: 1-19 while you imagine Brendan and his companions chanting the psalm. You may find that particular phrases touch you more deeply than others. Or you may find specific images, memories and emotions — perhaps even sounds and fragrances — associated with the different parts of the psalm. Make a mental note of these things.

After the monks conclude their prayer, allow their image to fade from your imagination as you become aware of the particular phrases and images from the psalm which touched you most deeply. Recall the emotions and memories — as well as any sounds or smells — evoked by the words of the psalm. Allow these key aspects of your prayer to linger on your mind and in your heart, making a mental note of any special feelings evoked by them.

When you are ready, speak with God in an open and informal manner about how the psalm expresses your own needs or desires — giving space for God to respond or to highlight different aspects of the psalm. Gradually allow your thoughts to recede as you focus on God's presence in your life and in the world around you.

[4]   When you are ready, take a moment to gather any important thoughts, emotions and memories from this meditation before concluding with this prayer:

O God of life, darken not to me your light,
O God of life, close not to me your joy,
O God of life, shut not to me your door,

171

O God of life, refuse not to me your mercy,
O God of life, quench toward me your wrath,
O God of life, crown me with your gladness,
O God of life, crown me with your gladness. Amen.

[5]   Again, take 5-10 minutes to reflect on this time of prayer before recording your preliminary reflections in your journal.

A repeated consideration of John 15

Verses 1 through 12

[1]   Again, feel your desire to live in God's goodness so you may use the many gifts God has given you. Feeling God's continuing care to you, open yourself to the immense love God shows for you. Then, ask God to grant you the gift of joy as you continue to walk in the presence of the Risen Christ through prayer and through service to others — whether in familiar circumstances or in those that require you to venture into the unknown.

As these desires fill your consciousness, allow all other concerns to fall aside as you focus on this specific time and place.

[2]   Then, again, take a moment to ponder the transformative power of Christ's resurrection — bringing life out of death, joy out of pain — before bringing to mind your earlier consideration of the allegory of the vine. Become aware of the moments from your earlier prayer that touched you most deeply, allowing particular phrases or images to linger in your consciousness as you ask Christ to illuminate your deepest needs and desires.

Ask Christ to call you through your imagination into a place where you could be a sign of his resurrection. As you look around, notice whether you are in the same place you were in your previous prayer or in a new and different one. Carefully observe the physical characteristics of this place and the people living there, listening to the conversations and other sounds around you.

Imagine Jesus approaching you. Greet him and allow him to welcome you into this place of his resurrection. Ask him where he lives in this place and allow him to show you. Then, as you walk or sit with him, hear Christ tell you the allegory of the vine as you slowly read John 15: 1-12. Afterward, speak with him about this allegory and its significance for you in this particular place.

[3]   After your conversation concludes, allow the image of Jesus to fade slowly from your consciousness. Feel the residue of consolation that remains after being with a close and dear friend as you conclude by offering this prayer:

> O God of life, darken not to me your light,
> O God of life, close not to me your joy,
> O God of life, shut not to me your door,
>   O God of life, refuse not to me your mercy,

O God of life, quench toward me your wrath,
O God of life, crown me with your gladness,
O God of life, crown me with your gladness. Amen.

[4]   Again, take 5-10 minutes to reflect on this time of prayer before recording your preliminary reflections in your journal.

An Application of the Senses

[1]   Again, feel your desire to live in God's goodness so you may use the many gifts God has given you. Feel God's continuing care as you open yourself to the immense love God shows for you and ask God to grant you the gift of joy as you continue to walk in the presence of the Risen Christ through prayer and through service to others — whether in familiar circumstances or in those that require you to venture into the unknown.

Then, focus on this moment as all other concerns fade away.

[2]   When you are ready, using your imagination, call to mind Brendan's visit to the Land of the Saints and his return home. Allow the images and words of this story to linger and then slowly fade from your consciousness. Consider the images and feelings evoked in you during your prayer, feeling God's presence in these memories and becoming aware of the specific sensations associated with each image.

Then, in turn, remember your recent prayers on Psalm 116, the appearance of the Risen Jesus at Lake Tiberias, and your conversation with Jesus about John 15. As these prayers enter your memory, make a mental note of which senses are most active. You may see an image or a color, hear a sound or a phrase, or smell a scent or a fragrance. You may even taste a flavor or feel a sensation on your skin.

Finally, relax and allow these various memories and experiences to quietly enter and leave your consciousness without being controlled — whether they are clear or diffuse, whether they come quickly or slowly. Linger on the sensory images and memories being evoked in you — noticing any images or colors, any sounds or phrases, any scents or fragrances, any flavors or physical sensations associated with each prayer.

[3]   When you are ready, become completely still and clear your mind of all thoughts and concerns. Watch as God forms a small image or object in your mind containing the most important gift you have been given during this particular time of prayer — the thought or awareness that you most need to carry with you into your life.

Reverently pick up the object or image, looking at it carefully and becoming aware of the divine presence contained within it. Take a moment to register what it looks like and how it feels in your hand. Then, feel the joy and confidence that comes from touching the presence of God as you accept this gift, offering a short prayer of gratitude while you relax into the pleasure of this moment.

[4]   Then, conclude by offering this prayer:

O God of life, darken not to me your light,
O God of life, close not to me your joy,
O God of life, shut not to me your door,
     O God of life, refuse not to me your mercy,
     O God of life, quench toward me your wrath,
     O God of life, crown me with your gladness,
O God of life, crown me with your gladness. Amen.

[5]   While your experiences are still fresh in your mind, record the most significant impressions or sensations from this time of prayer in your journal and thank God for the special gift you received from him.

Review

[1]   Remember your desire to walk in the presence of the Risen Christ through prayer and through service to others. Recall how you asked for the courage to follow the Risen Christ in familiar circumstances or in those that require you to venture into the unknown. Then, take a moment to allow the words, thoughts and feelings from your prayers during the last day or week to linger — on your mind and in your heart — before asking God to reveal His presence in these various memories.

[2]   Think about Brendan and his companions as they complete their pilgrimage. Remember the parts of the story that spoke most powerfully to you and think about how elements of this story resurfaced in your recent prayers on Psalm 116, the appearance of the Risen Jesus to the disciples at Lake Tiberias, and your conversation with Jesus about John 15. Ask God to help you understand these moments.

[3]   Consider your meditations on Psalm 116. Recall the most powerful images, phrases or feelings from your prayer. Ask yourself what gifts God gave to you through these moments, perhaps offering you new insights or perhaps affirming an important aspect of your faith. Ask yourself how God may be calling you to change through these moments, being as specific as possible.

Examine your disposition as you prayed, noting whether prayer came easily or with resistance. Recall the easiest moments in your prayer and any moments of joy you may have experienced. Remember also if you encountered any difficulty opening yourself to God or if you felt any sadness as you prayed. Ask God to help you understand why these feelings surfaced.

Bring to mind any moments when you added personal elements — familiar places or people from your life — or connected your prayers to other scriptures or spiritual writings. Ask yourself how these additions helped or hindered you as you prayed. Again, if you do not know why this happened, ask God to help you understand.

[4]   Ponder your contemplation of the appearance of the Risen Jesus at Lake Tiberias in John 21, allowing a mental picture of this event to form in your mind as you recall the perspective from which you experienced it. Then, review your prayer in the same way as your earlier reflection on Psalm 116.

[5]   Review your conversation with Jesus as you discussed John 15:

1-12. Again, allow a mental picture of this imaginative contemplation to form in your mind as you recall the details of this dialogue. Then, ponder your prayer in the same way as the earlier meditations on Psalm 116 and John 21.

[6]   Recall the ebb and flow of sensory impressions and feelings that marked your application of the senses. Isolate the most memorable moments and sensory impressions from your prayer and reflect on how God used these moments to give you a particular gift, perhaps offering you new insights or changing you in some way. Then, consider what you want to offer God in return for these moments.

[7]   Finally, remember the times when images or feelings from the readings of this day or week surfaced outside these prayer periods. Think about those moments or events in which God's presence or guidance was especially strong as well as any moments when you were struggling. Think about the most memorable aspects of these experiences, asking God to explain their significance.

[8]   Take a moment to allow the words, thoughts and feelings of these prayers to linger on your mind and in your heart. Then, conclude by asking for God's continued presence and guidance as you offer this prayer:

> Bless to me, O God,
>> Each thing my eyes see;
> Bless to me, O God,
>> Each sound my ears hear;
> Bless to me, O God,
>> Each odor that goes to my nostrils;
> Bless to me, O God,
>> Each taste that goes to my lips;
>> Each note that goes to my song,
>> Each ray that guides my way,
>> Each thing that I pursue,
>> Each lure that tempts my will,
>> The zeal that seeks my living soul,
> The Three that seek my heart,
>> The zeal that seeks my living soul,
> The Three that seek my heart. Amen.

[9]   After finishing these prayers, summarize the most significant moments, insights or desires from this last day or week in your journal before concluding these reflections in a short prayer of gratitude for the specific gifts or graces received during your prayers.

Conclusion

contemplating the mementos of grace

As you conclude your journey with Brendan and his companions, it is important that you prayerfully examine the spiritual gifts and graces you received during your travels. So, with this in mind, imagine yourself packing some traveling bags as you prepare to return to your normal routine after this special time of intense prayer. Allow significant moments from your retreat to coalesce into specific objects that you will be able to take with you and display in your home as reminders of your journey with Brendan and his companions. As you place each symbolic object into your luggage, take a moment to remember the particular spiritual gift or grace contained in it. Allow yourself to feel the pleasure you first experienced when you were given these souvenirs.

Also, take a moment to consider the feelings and concerns that you will leave behind as you complete your pilgrimage with Brendan and his companions. Allow these aspects of your prayers to coalesce into symbolic objects and imagine yourself either discarding them or giving them away — perhaps to God or to other people.

Then, feel a sense of gratitude emerging from your consideration of these many gifts and allow yourself to pray this traditional Gaelic prayer from Alexander Carmichael's *Carmina Gadelica*:

> *My God and my Chief,*
> *I seek you in the morning,*
> *My God and my Chief,*
> *I seek you this night.*
> *I am giving you my mind,*
> *I am giving you my will,*
> *I am giving you my wish,*
> *My soul everlasting and my body.*
>
> *May you be chieftain over me,*
> *May you be master unto me,*
> *May you be shepherd over me,*
> *May you be guardian unto me,*
> *May you be herdsmen over me,*

May you be guide unto me,
May you be with me, O Chief of chiefs,
Father everlasting and God of the heavens.
Amen.

Returning Home

God calls each of us to become instruments of love and hope to those around us — cultivating our "better angels" through service and prayer — but this also may require us to confront those people or social forces that might obstruct this vocation.

"The Burial of Saint Brendan"

by Padraic Colum

Nearing death, Brendan knew his body would offer both spiritual and material gifts that some people would try to appropriate for their own benefit. In Padraic Colum's "The Burial of Saint Brendan," the saint seeks to ensure that — even in death — he will be able to glorify God for the good of all rather than profit the selfish few.

On the third day from this (Saint Brendan said)
I will be where no wind that filled a sail
Has ever been, and it blew high or low:
For from this home-creek, from this body's close
I shall put forth: make ready, you, to go
With what remains to Cluan Hy-many,
For there my resurrection I'd have be.

But you will know how hard they'll strive to hold
This body o' me, and hold it for the place
Where I was bred, they say, and born and reared.
For they would have my resurrection here,
So that my sanctity might be matter shared
By every mother's child the tribeland polled
Who lived and died and mixed into the mould.

So you will have to use all canniness
To bring this body to its burial
When in your hands I leave what goes in clay;
The wagon that our goods are carried in —
Have it yoked up between the night and day,
And when the breath is from my body gone,
Bear body out, the wagon lay it on;

And cover it with gear that's taken hence —
"The goods of Brendan is what's here," you'll say

To those who'll halt you; they will pass you then:
Tinkers and tailors, soldiers, farmers, smiths,
You'll leave beside their doors — all those thwart men
For whom my virtue was a legacy
That they would profit in, each a degree —

As though it were indeed some chalice, staff,
Crozier or casket, that they might come to,
And show to those who chanced upon the way,
And have, not knowing how the work was done
In scrolls and figures and in bright inlay:
Whence came the gold and silver that they prize,
The blue enamels and the turquoises!

I, Brendan, had a name came from the sea —
I was the first who sailed the outer main,
And past all forelands and all fastnesses!
I passed the voiceless anchorets, their isles,
Saw the ice-palaces upon the seas,
Mentioned Christ's name to men cut off from men,
Heard the whales snort, and saw the Kraken!

And on a wide-branched, green, and glistening tree
Beheld the birds that had been angels erst:
Between the earth and heaven 'twas theirs to wing:
Fallen from High they were, but they had still
Music of Heaven's Court: I heard them sing:
Even now the island of the unbeached coast
I see, and hear the white, resplendent host!

For this they'd have my burial in this place,
Their hillside, and my resurrection be
Out of the mould that they with me would share.
But I have chosen Cluan for my ground
A happy place! Some grace came to me there:
And you, as you go towards it, to men say,
Should any ask you on that long highway:

"Brendan is here, who had great saints for friends:
Ita, who reared him on a mother's knee,
Enda, who from his fastness blessed his sail:
Then Brighid, she who had the flaming heart,
And Colum-cille, prime of all the Gael;
Gildas of Britain, wisest child of light."
And saying this, drive through the falling night.

As you reflect on this poem, take a moment to contemplate the graces and blessings you received from your spiritual journey with Saint Brendan and consider whether any of them might need to be protected against being misused, either by other people or by your own temptations. Then, in prayer, ask God to preserve the integrity of these spiritual gifts as well as your own handling of them.

Afterward, select specific moments, prayers and biblical selections in your retreat journal that encapsulate these spiritual gifts and record them in your workbook, grouping them around your specific concerns for each gift and noting the place in your journal where you received the gift. In the weeks after the retreat, repeat these contemplations or meditations in the manner described in "Nurturing the Courage of Pilgrims" while asking God to protect and preserve the grace you received during the retreat.

---

*   Padraic Colum, *The Poet's Circuits: Collected Poems of Ireland* (Dublin: Dolmen Press, 1981), pages 58-59.

Returning to Clonfert

some thoughts on Brendan's companions

While returning home to Clonfert from his journey brought Brendan renown, we hear nothing further of his companions. With a certain sadness, we realize that they are not even named in the telling of Brendan's journey. These companions rode on the back of the leviathan, were fed by God's special emissaries and saw angels singing as birds while traveling to the Land of the Saints with their abbot. And surely, just as Brendan did, they also took some souvenirs of that place — bits of fruit or precious stones — and brought them home where they may have shared them with others or quietly treasured them in private. Yet, we never hear any more of them after their return to Clonfert — whether they left the monastery again as missionaries or pilgrims, whether they chose to live as hermits or whether they quietly returned to the routines of monastic life. While Brendan is crowned with glory, his companions fade into the mists of anonymity.

Still, we know these holy companions received their share of graces during their travels. Inspired by Barrind's story and their love for Brendan, they generously and enthusiastically offered to join their abbot on his pilgrimage. But only through prayer would they have been able to remain faithful to that commitment during their difficult journey. Brendan's companions learned self-control and patience by working together within the tight confines of their boat, and their abbot's wisdom — shown in so many strange and dangerous situations — strengthened their ability to submit gently to his commands. They became kinder and more compassionate when they saw God's mercy towards terrible sinners or witnessed the deaths of their friends. Finally, they experienced a joyful sense of peace as they walked in the Land of the Saints before returning home. These are all fruits of God's holy Spirit, the hallmarks of a saintly life.

Nevertheless, while the spiritual gifts these monks received during their travels must have benefited their community in many significant ways, the contributions of these saintly companions remain hidden with their names. In all likelihood, Brendan's companions were respected — perhaps even admired — in their home community after their return home. But much of this recognition probably came from their association with the monastery's famous and saintly abbot, and at least some of those who came to them for blessings and spiritual guidance would have been seeking a surrogate for the saint. Still, even if these monks lived in the shadow of a great spiritual adventure, their lives would never have been reduced to this one event. God does not waste his gifts, and each of these hidden saints received the graces they needed to help build the kingdom of God through their own choices and actions.

So, it remains vitally important that we recognize the contributions of the many hidden saints who kept the Celtic spiritual traditions alive over the centuries. We certainly learn from the example and teachings of famous Celtic saints like Brendan, Brigid, Columba, Ita or Patrick — finding inspiration in the adventures and achievements of these great men and women — but we also need to recognize the spiritual vitality that surrounded these exemplary individuals, an aura of sanctity produced by generations of anonymous saints who practiced and preserved the Celtic traditions of prayer in private. These seemingly common and ordinary people (both in the ancient Celtic world and during the centuries after the Celtic churches faded into history) possessed an uncommon and exceptional spiritual life that helped empower the revival of Celtic spirituality in the last century or so, showing that the blessings and graces received through these ways of prayer were not limited to the better-known Celtic saints.

Recognizing the important contributions of these hidden saints also reminds us to acknowledge those people in our own lives who have shown us the face of Christ through their quiet gestures of kindness or faith — the hidden saints who humbly continue to build God's kingdom without fanfare — and encourages us to act with greater humility and generosity as we share the spiritual gifts we receive with others. Through their humble and unaffected testimonies, these men and women challenge us to accept the spiritual gifts and graces we receive to help build the kingdom of God and to share them with others, knowing that God's desires are being fulfilled through our actions and choices even when we are ignored or dismissed.

As you conclude your journey with Brendan and his companions, it is important that you devote some time to reviewing the gifts — both large and small — you received during your own prayerful pilgrimage and reflecting on which ones you might want to share with others as you strive to build the kingdom of God, even if you receive scant recognition for your efforts.

Again, locate specific moments, prayers and biblical selections in your retreat journal that encapsulate these spiritual gifts and record them in your workbook. Consider where these gifts might lead you, whether in service to familiar communities or in search of new and unknown places to serve God. Then, in prayer, ask God to nurture these gifts and preserve these holy desires.

In the weeks after the retreat, revisit these prayers in the manner described in "Nurturing the Courage of Pilgrims". Repeating the contemplation or meditation in which you first received a spiritual gift will further integrate its graces into the fabric of your life, but returning to the moments when you first received a specific spiritual gift through an application of the senses may intensify your gratitude for God's generosity toward you. So, consider your needs and use the technique best suited to them.

further reflections and exercises

After completing this journey with Brendan and his companions, you will find it helpful to consider the spiritual gifts you received during your pilgrimage. Some of the benefits from this time of prayer may be readily apparent, allowing you to embrace them with enthusiasm. Others may remain obscured from your full view, obliging you to approach them with caution. Still others may rest below the surface of your consciousness, causing feelings of anxiety or concern as they begin to evoke unfamiliar ideas and impulses. In whatever form they manifest themselves, the gifts and graces of your travels with Brendan and his companions invite you to be transfigured into a sign of God's loving presence in the world.

With rare exceptions, this transformation takes time. It is easy to make promises in dedicated times of intense prayer that may be difficult for you to fulfill amid the many demands of your daily life. So, God's spiritual gifts and graces often behave like seeds placed in well-prepared soil. God plants an aspect of his divine plan of salvation in you and provides the nourishment needed for this seed to germinate, sending tendrils out in a search for further nutrients that will allow it to take root before blossoming for all to see. Like a careful gardener, God knows your unique capabilities and plants in you the seeds that are most able to be nourished and sustained. Still, you must actively nurture these seeds of grace through your prayers and in your actions.

Nourishing the Graces of God

So, as you nourish the gifts you received during your time with Brendan and his companions, you should be consoled by the knowledge that God's benevolence remains constant but be concerned by the realization that your ability to nurture God's gifts remains vulnerable. Indeed, during this time of transition, the generosity of spirit that opened you to God's beneficence also may expose you to distractions and temptations that could lead you away from God. For this reason, you need to remain vigilant during this very delicate time and avoid making any significant or life-changing decisions while helping the graces of your recent prayers mature and complete their work in you. With these thoughts in mind, you may find it helpful to keep a journal as you:

• On a daily basis, monitor your thoughts and emotions by making an examen. You may want to continue using the Celtic examens provided in this book or find other versions through an online search.

• On at least a weekly basis, repeat one of the most significant scriptural selections from your earlier prayers using the instructions associated with them in the retreat. You also may choose to revisit these moments from your retreat through an application of the senses.

• On at least a monthly basis, contemplate your "mementos of grace" using the method described in the self-guided retreat's conclusion.

• Finally, when your spiritual or emotional disposition becomes especially intense, you should make an imaginative contemplation on a scriptural topic that mirrors your feelings (e.g., the openness of Samuel in 1 Samuel 3: 1-10, the resistance of Jonah in Jonah 1: 1-17 or the discouragement of Elijah in 1 Kings 19: 3-13).

Note: Do not allow these prayers to become a burden. Instead, approach them as an opportunity to quietly re-engage the seminal aspects of your pilgrimage with Brendan and his companions. Still, it is important to chronicle your experiences as the gifts of your earlier prayers deepen and mature — without making any life-choices based on them.

Nurturing the Courage of Pilgrims

After at least four months of gentle prayer, you may begin to consider any spiritual leadings calling you to change your life in a substantial way (e.g., committing to a new form of service, participation in a prayer group, joining a religious organization, etc.). Whether these impulses ask you to become more involved in your existing community or call you to leave familiar surroundings, they involve a journey into the unknown and invite you to revisit the themes of your earlier prayers. With confidence in God's presence and protection — seeds of grace planted and nurtured during your travels with Brendan and his companions — you will be able to make this pilgrimage with courage and conviction.

Still, to help you clarify this new spiritual journey, you may want to download *Nurturing the Courage of Pilgrims* using the instructions at the beginning of the resources section of this book. This PDF booklet contains reflections and spiritual exercises organized around the three spiritual ideals of Brendan's foster-mother and life-long mentor, Saint Ita of Killeedy: "true faith in God with a pure heart," "a simple life with a grateful spirit," and "generosity inspired by charity." *Nurturing the Courage of Pilgrims* also contains considerations on the social aspects of the spiritual life (sacred citizenship) as well as the challenges of finding creative ways of sharing your faith journey with others (articulate witness).

Resources for Private Prayer

Introduction

In this section, you will find a link to online digital materials designed to accompany this retreat as well as resources designed to help you cultivate habits of prayer that will enrich your experience while following the journey of Brendan and his companions:

- "Digital Resources" provides a link to online materials intended to assist individuals as they prepare for this retreat or to reflect on their experiences after completing it. These include a mini-course introducing the types of Ignatian prayer used in the retreat as well as a PDF booklet intended to help you reflect upon the spiritual gifts of the retreat and the leadings evoked by these graces.
- "On Holy Ground" suggests three short rituals that you might use to consecrate your prayer. These spiritual gestures will create a mental "common space" that unifies the different times and places in which you pray, strengthening your ability to create good prayer habits and easing your entry into the silence and solitude of contemplation.
- The two Celtic examens highlight God's activity in your day. "Making a Morning Caim" presents a Celtic encircling prayer in which you look forward to the coming day while the "An Evening Prayer of Remembrance" looks back at the events and people you encountered during your day in a litany of gratitude. These prayerful reviews should focus on the concrete expressions of God's love in your daily life, equipping you — on a direct and emotional level — to discern God's desires in your life and to amend your life to be in harmony with them.

Note: In a daily life retreat, these examens stand alone and take no more than fifteen minutes each. But, in seclusion (where much of your day is devoted to formal prayer), you might find it helpful to integrate these prayers into your daily preparation and review exercises.

- The descriptions of imaginative contemplation and the application of the senses provide you with a clear and easy to follow structure for these two types of Ignatian prayer. You will find it helpful to refer to these materials as you prepare your prayer until you are familiar with these techniques. But you also should feel free to adapt these guidelines as you discern your particular ways of imagining the events in the retreat's contemplations and of speaking comfortably with

Jesus about your experiences.

Digital Resources

for this self-guided retreat

The digital resources for this book may be found at:

http://www.resources.silentheron.net

These include:
- • an audio mini-course introducing the Ignatian prayer styles used during this retreat: the imaginative contemplation, the application of the senses and the examen
- • *Nurturing the Courage of Pilgrims*, the follow-up booklet for this retreat (described in the "Returning Home" section)

On Holy Ground

---

rituals for creating a sacred space

The consequences of incorporating personal rituals into our prayer often exceed our expectations. The consistent use of private rituals helps us develop bodily habits that allow us to more quickly put aside our daily concerns and enter into a prayerful conversation with our Creator. But these rituals also remind us that we are invoking protection and guidance while seeking communion with a loving God. With each successive act of ritual, we invite God to consecrate our time with him and reconfirm our desire that he transform us into signs of his presence in the world.

With these goals in mind, you may find one or more of the following three rituals (using traditional Gaelic prayers selected from Alexander Carmichael's *Carmina Gadelica*) helpful:

#1 — A Trinitarian Act of Humility

Note: For this ritual, place three candles at the focal point of your prayer space — along with an image of the Trinity (e.g., a triskele or an icon), if you like. You also will need some matches or a long lighter.

• After relaxing into your prayer space, light the candles while reciting this prayer:
I am bending my knee
(lighting the first candle)
in the eye of the Father who created me,
(lighting the second candle)
in the eye of the Son who died for me,
(lighting the third candle)
in the eye of the Spirit who cleansed me,
in love and desire.
• After completing your prayer, as you prepare to leave your prayer space, extinguish the candles in the same order you originally lit them while repeating the following prayer:
I am bending my knee
in the eye of the Father who created me,

(extinguishing the first candle)
in the eye of the Son who died for me,
(extinguishing the second candle)
in the eye of the Spirit who cleansed me,
(extinguishing the third candle)
in love and desire. Amen.

#2 — A Personal Caim (Encircling Prayer)

Note: *This ritual does not require any objects, but you may want to use a crucifix or other image of Jesus as the focal point of your prayer space.*

• After becoming comfortable, open your hands — palms up — in front of you or pick up and hold the image of Jesus. Then, looking at your palms or the image, offer the following prayer:

O Lord, who brought me from the rest of last night
Unto the joyous light of this day,
Bring me from the new light of this day
Unto the guiding light of eternity.

• Now, allowing an image to form in your imagination as you slowly say:

The shape of Christ be towards me,
The shape of Christ be from me,
The shape of Christ be before me,
The shape of Christ be behind me,
The shape of Christ be over me,
The shape of Christ be under me,
The shape of Christ be with me,
The shape of Christ be around me.

• When you are finished, return the image of Jesus to its place or move your hands to where you will hold them during prayer.
• After you finish your prayer, pick up and hold the image of Jesus or open your hands in front of you as you pray:

O Lord, bring me from the new light of this day
Unto the guiding light of eternity.
Oh! from the new light of this day
Unto the guiding light of eternity. Amen.

• Wait a moment in silence after the prayer. Then, close your hands or replace the image of Jesus before leaving.

#3 — A Veneration of the Cross

Note: In this ritual, the focal point for your prayer space should include a candle placed before a cross or crucifix. You also will need some matches or a lighter.

- After calming yourself, make the sign of the cross while saying:
        In the name of the King of life,
        In the name of the Christ of love,
        In the name of the Holy Spirit,
        The triune of my strength.
- Then, light the candle before continuing with this prayer:
        May the cross of the crucifixion tree
        Upon the wounded back of Christ
        Deliver me from distress,
        From death and from spells.

        The cross of Christ without fault,
        All outstretched toward me;
        O God, bless me!
- After concluding your prayer period, repeat the following prayer while you extinguish the candle:
        May the cross of the crucifixion tree
        Upon the wounded back of Christ
        Deliver me from distress,
        From death and from spells.

        The cross of Christ without fault,
        All outstretched toward me;
        O God, bless me!
- Then, make the sign of the cross as you say:
        In the name of the King of life,
        In the name of the Christ of love,
        In the name of the Holy Spirit,
        The triune of my strength. Amen.

Making a Morning Caim

a prayerful consideration of the coming day

[1]   Focus on this present moment and allow all other concerns or problems to fade from your consciousness. Then, become aware of your desire to know the fullness of God's love for you — and to feel his continuing compassion and guidance — as you quietly affirm God's redemptive presence in you and in the world around you.

[2]   Consider your life. Bring to mind the times when you do not reflect God's goodness, the times when you squander or misuse the gifts he has given to you, and the times when you feel abandoned by God. Become aware of your desire to live in God's goodness as well as your desire to properly use the many gifts he has given you.

[3]   Pray for the grace to see God's action in your life more clearly, to understand his desires for you more accurately, to respond to his guidance to you more generously. Pray also that others in the world might see, understand and respond to God's guidance in their lives.

[4]   Now, imagine the coming day, seeing God's love enfolding and encircling every situation. Feel God's love touch you in the depths of your being, expressing his desire to share his creation with you in the coming day. Ask God to bless your day, the people and creatures you will meet in it, and those who are close to your heart.

• Then, see God in all the events and people of the coming morning. Feel his loving presence surrounding, protecting and guiding you as you imagine the moments when you expect to be alone during this morning and when you expect to be with other people. Feel God's love pervade your home, your work and your travels as you ask him to encircle the events and people of this morning with his love, saying:

The compassing of God be on you,
The compassing of the God of life.

• Imagine the events and people of the coming midday. Again, feel God's presence surrounding, protecting and guiding you as you see the moments when you expect to be alone and when you expect to be with other people. As you ask him to encircle the events and people of this midday with his love, saying:

The compassing of Christ be on you,
The compassing of the Christ of love.

• Envision the coming afternoon, seeing God's presence in the times when you are alone and when you are with others. Hear his voice speak to you in all these events and people as you ask God to encircle them with his love, saying:

> *The compassing of Spirit be on you,*
> *The compassing of the Spirit of Grace.*

• Finally, see the coming evening. Feel God's love pervade the moments when you expect to be alone and when you expect to be with other people before asking him to encircle them with his love, saying:

> *The compassing of the Three be on you,*
> *The compassing of the Three preserve you,*
> *The compassing of the Three preserve you.*

[5]   As you allow these images to ebb and flow in your consciousness, make a mental note of your emotional responses to the people and events you expect to encounter during the coming day, quietly affirming your desire to live in God's goodness. Then, become aware of your need for God's continuing care and guidance so you may properly use the many gifts he has given you in these circumstances — and in the unexpected events of this day.

[6]   When you are ready, conclude by offering this traditional prayer:

> *God, bless to me the new day,*
> *Never vouchsafed to me before;*
> *It is to bless your own presence*
> *You have given me this time, O God.*
> *Bless my eyes,*
> *may my eyes bless all they see;*
> *I will bless my neighbor,*
> *May my neighbor bless me.*
> *God, give me a clean heart,*
> *let me not from sight of your eye. Amen.*

An Evening Prayer of Remembrance

venerating God's presence in the passing day

[1]   Become completely focused on this present moment and allow all other concerns or problems to dissolve from your consciousness. Become aware of God's goodness and of the many gifts that God has given to you, quietly acknowledging God's sustaining power in your life and in the world around you.

[2]   Consider your life. Bring to mind the times when you do not reflect God's goodness, the times when you squander or misuse the gifts God has given to you, and the times when you feel abandoned by God. Become aware of your desire to live in God's goodness and quietly affirm your desire to properly use the many gifts God has given you, asking for God's continuing guidance to help you achieve this goal.

[3]   Become aware of the need — both in you and in the world around you — for God's healing and redemptive presence.

• Open yourself to that divine presence as you ponder and pray the words of this traditional prayer:

I am bending my knee
    In the eye of the Father who created me,
    In the eye of the Son who purchased me,
    In the eye of the Spirit who cleansed me,
In friendship and affection.

• Then, pray for the grace to see God's action in your life more clearly, to understand God's desires for you more accurately, and to respond to God's guidance to you more generously. Pray also that others in the world might see, understand and respond to God's guidance in their lives.

[4]   Now, review this day in your memory, allowing yourself to feel God's presence in its events and emotions.

• Remember waking this morning. Recall whether you awoke easily or with difficulty, calling to mind how you felt — whether you were happy, sad, relaxed or tense. Make a mental note of whether you felt God close to you or distant from you. Take a moment to consider these things, acknowledging the shaping presence of God in the beginning of the day, as you say:

I am bending my knee

In friendship and affection.

• Recall your preparations for the day. Remember whether you dressed quickly or slowly, calling to mind your thoughts and feelings. Ask yourself whether God was on your mind as you prepared for this day. Take a moment to consider any feelings that these memories evoke in you, acknowledging the shaping presence of God in them, as you say:

I am bending my knee
In friendship and affection.

• Bring to mind your morning. Recall those moments when you were alone and when you were with other people. Recall the emotions you felt during the morning hours, allowing specific feelings to connect to the things you did as well as the things about which you thought or talked. Ask yourself how God was present to you this morning. Take a moment to consider these images and feelings, acknowledging the shaping presence of God in them, as you say:

I am bending my knee
In friendship and affection.

• Call to mind what you did at midday, remembering those moments when you were alone and when you were with other people, becoming aware of any emotions associated with specific things you did or things about which you thought or talked. Ask yourself about the ways in which God was present to you or on your mind at midday. Take a moment to consider these images and feelings, acknowledging the shaping presence of God in them, as you say:

I am bending my knee
In friendship and affection.

• Remember your afternoon, recalling those moments when you were alone and when you were with other people. Recall the emotions you felt during the afternoon, particularly if they are connected to specific things you did or about which you thought or talked. Ask yourself how God was present to you this afternoon. Take a moment to consider these images and feelings, acknowledging the shaping presence of God in them, as you say:

I am bending my knee
In friendship and affection.

• Recall your evening, remembering those moments when you were alone and when you were with other people. Become aware of any emotions you felt during the evening hours as you consider the things you did as well as the things about which you thought or talked.

Ask yourself how God revealed his presence to you this evening. Take a moment to consider these images and feelings, acknowledging the shaping presence of God in them, as you say:

> *I am bending my knee*
> *In friendship and affection.*

• Consider the present moment. Become aware of your feelings and your current sense of God's presence. Take a moment to consider these feelings, acknowledging the shaping presence of God in this moment, as you say:

> *I am bending my knee*
> *In friendship and affection.*

[5]   Allow all the images and memories to flow freely in your consciousness, feeling God's presence in them. Make a mental note of your emotional responses to these images and memories as they ebb and flow. Then, become aware once again of your desire to live in God's goodness as you quietly affirm your desire to properly use the many gifts he has given you and ask for his continued guidance as you try to achieve this goal.

[6]   When you are ready, conclude with this traditional prayer:

> *Through your own Anointed One, O God,*
> *Bestow upon us fullness in our need.*
>> *Love towards God,*
>> *The affection of God,*
>> *The smile of God,*
>> *The wisdom of God,*
>> *The grace of God,*
>> *The fear of God*
> *To do in the world of the Three,*
> *As angels and saints*
> *Do in heaven;*
>> *Each shade and light,*
>> *Each day and night,*
>> *Each time in kindness,*
>> *Give us your Spirit. Amen.*

Imaginative Contemplation

connecting imagination and prayer during your retreat

In his *Spiritual Exercises,* Ignatius of Loyola (the founder of the Ignatian spiritual tradition) lays out a basic pattern for the imaginative contemplation. This involves asking God to give you a specific grace during your time of prayer, carefully reviewing the basic elements of a particular scriptural episode related to your spiritual needs, and then using your imagination to enter into those events. For Ignatius, it is important that you allow your imagination (and not your pre-existing desires or expectations) to guide you into prayer — opening an emotional and spiritual space for the Holy Spirit to bridge the divide between your unique personal experience and the universal message revealed in the scripture. In many cases, Ignatius also suggests you discuss the fruits of your contemplation in a casual imaginary conversation with Jesus before concluding with a formal prayer.

Ignatius also emphasized the careful review of prayer afterward, listening for patterns of openness and resistance in your conversations with God. Humbly listening to these clues in your prayer — and in your daily life through the examen — sustains a quiet movement toward becoming what Ignatius called a "contemplative in action" as you learn to recognize the patterns of God's presence in every aspect of your life.

With this in mind, you may find it helpful to use the following approach to your prayer during the retreat:

1. Begin your prayer by relaxing into the moment. Take time to center yourself and become completely aware of your feelings and thoughts in the present. When you have properly prepared yourself, take a moment to consider the specific gifts you wish to receive through this particular time of prayer and present these needs to God.

Note: You also should allow space for God to help you discern other spiritual and emotional needs you might have, remembering that these leadings will come from a loving and nurturing God.

2. Read the scriptural selection you will be using in your prayer. Do this slowly and meditatively, allowing it to seep deep into your consciousness.

As you review the passage of Scripture that you will use during this time of prayer, visualize the main elements of the story that is being told and the physical environment in which that story takes place. Take your time to slowly see the people involved in the story, their surroundings and objects relevant to their actions, and what they are doing.

Note: It is important to make certain that you understand the key elements of the story and their significance as you compose in your imagination the contemplation for a specific prayer period.

3. When you are ready, imagine yourself in the story being told to you. Become aware of whether or not you participate directly in the events of the story or observe them. Become aware of what the environment feels like and how you are affected by the different people and events of the story being told to you in prayer.

Depending on how you use your imagination, this can mean many different things. Some people are able to "see" very strong visual images from the scriptural story while others "hear" the conversations in the passage and still others have strong emotional impressions during imaginative contemplations. You will need to find — and trust — your own way of imagining yourself in the scripture passage you want to contemplate.

Allow your imagination to guide you during the contemplation and do not try to control the images of the prayer. Sometimes, a distraction may reveal powerful insights or hidden desires you want to share with God. Or if you find yourself expanding on the story at the heart of your prayer — by connecting it to other scriptural passages or adding details from your own life — these "expansions" may be God's way of communicating with you.

Note: Still, do not strain to hold onto your prayer if you find yourself unable to stay in the imaginative realm. Feel free to refer to the scriptural account (or any notes you prepared for your prayer) if necessary, taking a few deep breaths after putting these materials aside and allowing your imagination to guide you forward from the point where you became distracted.

4. After completing the contemplation, allow your personal needs and desires to come to the surface of your consciousness. Then,

gather them and express them in an informal and friendly conversation with Christ. Speak as you would to a close friend, being certain to allow space for Christ to speak to you about his needs as well.

Ignatius called this prayer the colloquy, an exercise of the imagination in which you share the deepest desires of your heart with a loving and interested God. Like the Celtic saints, Ignatius believed that God actively engages us — in our prayer and in the world around us — in a conversation intended to fulfill God's desires for a redeemed creation.

Note: Sometimes, this conversation constitutes the bulk of a *prayer period.*

5. Conclude your imaginative contemplation with a short formal prayer, such as Lord's Prayer or one of your own favorites.

6. Review your prayer. Write down the significant moments from your contemplation and the colloquy shortly after leaving the space in which you prayed. You might find it helpful to compare notes from different contemplations since this will help you understand the ways your imagination guides you in prayer. Also, by helping you mark the growing presence of God in your life, these acts of review will nurture your capacity to discern God's will for you and deepen your gratitude for God's loving presence in your life.

The Application of the Senses

a quiet prayer of emotional and sense memories

The primary form of imaginative contemplation outlined by Ignatius of Loyola in his *Spiritual Exercises* reflects his active and vigorous spirituality. It requires that you use your thoughts, feelings and imagination to enter into an active conversation with God. But, also in his *Spiritual Exercises*, Ignatius suggests a very different type of imaginative prayer which he called the "application of the senses." It is a prayer of memory in which you gently listen for God's voice in the emotions and physical sensations of your earlier prayers.

Ignatius of Loyola places the application of the senses at the end of the day, when you might be tired or need to relax. For this reason, the application of the senses might be considered the Ignatian counterpart to traditional compline, a night prayer intended to draw together the strands of one's contemplation during the course of the preceding day. However, unlike the forms of Christian contemplation which try to empty the consciousness of sensual images, this prayer uses the memory in concert with your emotions and five physical senses to gently reflect on God's presence in you and in your world.

With this in mind, you might find it helpful to use the following approach when making an application of the senses:

1. Begin your prayer by relaxing into the moment. Take time to center yourself and become completely aware of your feelings and thoughts in the present. When you have properly prepared yourself, allow the memories of your earlier prayers to ebb and flow in your consciousness without trying to guide or control your reminiscences.

2. When a particular moment of prayer comes into your consciousness, remember the grace or spiritual gift you desired in the initial prayer. Then gently consider in turn the images, sounds, smells, flavors and physical feelings associated with your earlier prayer. Recognize that one of your senses may dominate the way that you imagine a moment in your prayer, so allow this sense to "lead" you into the events of your prayer — and toward other sense memories.

Note: *Allow these sense images from your memory to surface in your consciousness without trying to control or interpret them as they emerge. Simply find pleasure as these images and feelings come to you in what has been described as "a gentle soak in meaningful impressions". It is a highly visceral and, very often, pleasant experience.*

3. Repeat this process with another prayer experience as it comes into your consciousness. Without constraining your thoughts, allow different memories from your earlier prayer to ebb and flow as you re-experience the feelings associated with different prayers.

4. When you are ready, allow these various memories and feelings to fade from your consciousness as you allow an image or object that encapsulates all these experiences to form in your mind. Take some time to speak with God about the meaning or significance of this object.

5. Conclude your imaginative contemplation with a short formal prayer, such as the Lord's Prayer or one of your own favorites.

6. Write down any significant memories or feelings from this prayer shortly after leaving the space in which you prayed. You might find it helpful to compare notes from different applications of the senses since this will help you understand the ways your imagination guides you in prayer. Also, these acts of review will nurture your capacity to discern the growing presence of God in your life.

Printed in Great Britain
by Amazon

49272697R00130